Praise for *The Anti-Racist Organization*

'We live in a world built on white supremacy and white privilege. Shereen has written a clear, wonderfully easy-to-read book that tells us what we can do about it. From diagnosis to reflection to action, *The Anti-Racist Organization* is a blueprint for change and offers a challenge for us to see each other's humanity. Whether you're a leader or an employee, white or Black, I believe you'll gain a lot by reading it.'

Tony Langham, Executive Chair and Co-founder, Lansons

'As a finance leader and a white woman, Shereen's words inspire me every day to keep pushing to bring down structural racism both in business and society at large. Shereen is voicing the conversations that your Black and brown colleagues are having behind closed doors every day. Stand up, listen and act. Be part of the change.'

Karla Smith, Lead Finance Director, Ogilvy UK

'This book weighed heavily on me, as it should. It's unapologetic, enlightening and yet practical. If you are truly interested in becoming an anti-racist organization, you won't just read this once, but will refer back to it again and again.'

Dr Jane Brearley, Founder & CEO, Intent Health LTD

'This book is an extension of Shereen's passion, honesty and ability to open your thought process and understanding of the world as it equates to racism. You will question your long standing assumptions/beliefs and/or unconscious thought processes. If you are serious about understanding racism, this is not a "maybe" read but a "must" read for anyone to actively engage in changing the narrative.'

Mary-Anne Price, HR Director, England Golf

'This is an honest, thought-provoking book that takes you on a journey of discomfort that leaves you reflecting on your personal and professional relationship with race and racism.'

Cheryl Samuels, Deputy Director of Workforce Transformation, NHS England

'What Shereen critiques here is powerful and needed, cuts no punches and tells it straight up; that is what we all need now more than ever before in this crazy world. I urge you to grab this book and read it and read it again and if you're like me you will need to breathe and start at the beginning all over.'

Margot Slattery, Group Head of Diversity & Inclusion , ISS World Services

'Shereen enlightens the reader with practical steps for those truly motivated to build an Anti-Racist Organization. This book should be mandatory reading for all CEOs.'

Matthew Phelan, Co-Founder, The Happiness Index

'Shereen writes clearly and simply for readers to grasp. If after reading this book you aren't motivated to take transformational action or alter how you do this work, then you need to read it again.'

*Cornell Verdeja-Woodson, Director of Diversity, Equity,
and Belonging, Headspace Health*

The Anti-Racist Organization

The Anti-Racist Organization

Dismantling Systemic Racism in the Workplace

Shereen Daniels

Registered office
John Wiley & Sons, Inc., 111 River Street, Hoboken, NJ 07030, USA
John Wiley & Sons Ltd, The Atrium, Southern Gate, Chichester, West Sussex, PO19 8SQ, United Kingdom

Editorial Office
John Wiley & Sons Ltd, The Atrium, Southern Gate, Chichester, West Sussex, PO19 8SQ, United Kingdom

For details of our global editorial offices, customer services, and more information about Wiley products visit us at www.wiley.com.

Wiley also publishes its books in a variety of electronic formats and by print-on-demand. Some content that appears in standard print versions of this book may not be available in other formats.

Library of Congress Cataloging-in-Publication Data

Names: Daniels, Shereen, author.
Title: The anti-racist organization : dismantling systemic racism in the workplace / Shereen Daniels.
Description: Hoboken, NJ : John Wiley & sons, Inc., 2022. | Includes index.
Identifiers: LCCN 2021059123 (print) | LCCN 2021059124 (ebook) | ISBN 9781119880622 (cloth) | ISBN 9781119880646 (adobe pdf) | ISBN 9781119880639 (epub)
Subjects: LCSH: Racism in the workplace—United States. | Discrimination in employment—United States. | Diversity in the workplace—United States. | United States—Race relations.
Classification: LCC HF5549.5.R23 D36 2022 (print) | LCC HF5549.5.R23 (ebook) | DDC 658.30089/00973—dc23
LC record available at https://lccn.loc.gov/2021059123
LC ebook record available at https://lccn.loc.gov/2021059124

Cover Design: Wiley
Cover Image: © Yevhenii Orlov/Getty Images

SKY10034617_052722

To
Black colleagues in every shape and size of organization.
You are not broken.
You don't need fixing.
You matter.
I dedicate this book to you.

Contents

Preface

Dismantling racism isn't about who's perfect. It isn't about who's nailed it. It isn't about who's getting public accolades.

It's about who's got the moral courage to do some introspective reflection, and then go, 'You know what, this isn't right. This is not good enough and we're going to be part of the solution.'

Shereen Daniels

How to Read This Book

Read any traditional marketing 'bible' or listen to the advice of seasoned sales professionals and they will all tell you the same thing. When writing a book, particularly a business one, aim to solve the problems of your readers. Make sure you speak their language.

You must resonate with them.

You should make them feel like every word you write is aimed personally at them and that you, and you alone, hold the key to their solving their problems.

Position yourself as the expert.

Reinforce your credibility.

Centre them and their needs.

Always.

When some contacts in my network knew I was writing this book, they had some words of advice along similar lines but specific to the subject matter:

Be careful you don't take things too far in what you write about. You don't want to alienate potential customers.

You have to know how to play the game and meet people where they are.

White people are tired of having racism shoved down their throats. We didn't create these problems.

The problem is that change takes time. You need to be more patient and ease people into this rather than hitting them over the head.

Don't forget to focus on the good work that organizations have done. It's not all bad news. Could you highlight that in your book, do you think?

Maybe you're someone who has said or thought something akin to these ideas, in relation to this subject matter in other contexts.

The Anti-Racist Organization isn't a book that panders to whiteness or seeks to make the subject palatable for decision makers. It isn't one that gently cajoles leaders into action, creating a smooth, risk-free path to racial equity. Nor does it seek to convince anyone that racism is a 'thing' and why you should care enough to do differently.

We are beyond this now.

Prioritising the comfort of white leaders is partly why organizations are still microcosms of racism and discrimination. Through ignorance, fear and a lack of addressing the root causes, we have continued to uphold and preserve environments that work for the white majority yet are harmful to Black colleagues.

We cannot disrupt and dismantle what we seek to change if we retreat at the first signs of discomfort, whether that's within ourselves or in our teams.

As someone who is personally impacted by the very topic I advise on, I am no longer motivated by the need to be accepted by the majority, by the demand to maintain the status quo or by the desire to avoid disrupting the apple cart.

I, and millions of people like me, have done that. It has gotten us nowhere. Because here we are, still missing from many corridors of power and still building business cases to dismantle systemic racism.

What to Expect

Each chapter is a quick read that, although light in words, contains considerable content that will prompt questions to which you thought you knew all the answers. You are unlikely to see the world in quite the same way again. You are likely to flinch at times, and that's okay. It's to be expected.

Whilst this book is addressed to you, I'm centring your Black colleagues and the issues at hand that uniquely impact on their experiences in the workplace:

Racism.
Not diversity.
Not inclusion.
Not belonging.

Specifics matter, and it's important we hold the line to ensure that when we are talking about systemic racism, we don't bend and weave with the language we use.

I am compassionate and empathetic in my ongoing challenges to you, because – if you join me – we are walking the same path: using curiosity and introspection to advance racial equity, challenging the deeply held beliefs and values about who we are, what is the leadership legacy we want to leave behind and examining our personal relationship with race and racism.

Detractors believe that to consistently talk about racism, how it shows up, what we should do differently is to stoke fires of division. That it's anti-white, not professional, inhumane.

I disagree.

Creating environments that mirror the unequal, inequitable aspects of society is inhumane.

Ignoring the lived experiences of colleagues because they are a minority in your organization is inhumane.

Having systems and practices that reward behaviour that excludes people because of their skin colour and other characteristics is inhumane.

Addressing the root cause of systemic racism, drawing attention to where it shows up and how you can take intentional steps to make a difference is one of the most rewarding and impactful cultural transformation programmes you can ever embark on.

You are doing when most are still talking.

That's humanity.

I Did Not Wake up Like This

You could be mistaken for believing that the confidence I have in addressing these issues head on has always been there. You might think to commend me for my bravery and steadfast approach in speaking truth to power. It may seem that my strength of character and openness about advocating for Black people first is the culmination of a life-long journey that can be traced to some point in my distant past.

The truth is, I didn't wake up like this – not with this level of insight. It was not really an objective decision to channel my HR and leadership experience into advancing racial equity.

For years I had held tight to a belief that we cannot bite the hand that feeds us. I felt obligated to demonstrate gratitude for any and all opportunities that were coming my way, because they weren't typical for people who look like me. I operated from a place of fear, recognising that no matter how senior I got, my position was precarious to many of my colleagues, peers and managers. I was just 'the Black girl in HR'.

I was taught to turn the other cheek, not to show emotion lest I be typecast as an 'angry Black woman' in the workplace. To show a bit more emotion meant I risked intimidating others, particularly those people who 'aren't used to being around Black people'. I sensed pressure to be held as the exemplary Black person who doesn't make excuses and to be seen as the professional who never 'plays the race card'.

You've done so well. Clearly racism hasn't affected you like it has other people. Why do you think that is?

Various versions of this statement made me realise the cost of silence – the cost of saying little to nothing about how I really felt, the cost of assimilating and integrating into majority white spaces that were threatened by my presence because I was different. And if there was more than one Black person, well, what's going on here?

Every time certain situations kept happening, I rationalised them away. He didn't mean it. She was just upset. Maybe I'm reading it wrong. I wasn't conciliatory enough, I was too assertive, I wasn't 'soft' enough, I was too intimidating.

The reality was that I was afraid, and ashamed of my fear. For all my big talk and bravado, I always stopped short of being myself, because I didn't want to run of the risk of being rejected – by white people, who, in my eyes, held all the power, whilst I and people like me held none.

I could never say this to my colleagues, but I knew. I knew that I lived, worked and played in a society that meant when push came to shove, my life, my dreams, my aspirations didn't matter as much. And despite how much I wished things were different, there wasn't a lot I could do about it.

I had no choice.

Make the best of what I was dealt with, don't let it stop me.

Work that bit harder.

Prove them wrong.

Accept that nothing can change.

On 25 May 2020, the same day George Floyd was murdered, a white woman named Amy Cooper was walking her dog in Central Park in New York City. I'm sure she had no idea that she would soon become the symbolic embodiment of a woman who weaponised her race, all because a Black man reprimanded her for letting her dog run free in an area where leashing is required. Amy called the police, relying on her privilege in being able to do so, knowing she would be believed and the likely outcome facing the Black man she abused. Her phone calls were made mere hours before George Floyd's murder in Minneapolis by a police officer.

Amy Cooper was my reckoning point.

I saw with absolute clarity that I had spent so much of my life surrounded by the male and female versions of Amy Cooper. There were Amy Coopers in my school and universities. I led teams with Amy Coopers, was managed by Amy Coopers, even had friendships and romantic relationships with versions of Amy Coopers.

In that moment it dawned on me that for all those years when I thought the problem was with me, it wasn't. Yet my silence through fear and discomfort meant I was complicit.

Yes, it is possible to be impacted by racism and at the same time be an agent of its existence.

What did I have to be afraid of?

That by speaking out I would be ostracised and rejected.

That I would become that Black woman who always talks about racism.

That I would become that Black person who makes people feel uncomfortable in sharing my experiences of discrimination and how it's affected me.

That the model image of the Black professional I had spent almost twenty years cultivating would crumble away, and the person I really was and who I really wanted to be would be 'too Black' to be accepted by the majority.

And where would that leave me? Too often it's assumed that racism is cut and dried. Black and white. But it isn't. It's uncomfortable, messy and complex.

No one helped me untangle the guilt, shame and embarrassment I felt at having never said anything (or at least very little) when I was in the corporate world, at not actively being part of dismantling racism, at not doing more to support, champion and advocate for other Black people. Systemic racism is a system that divides, even within those of us who share the same ethnicity. Head down and get on with it. I don't have the time, energy or space to take on other people's struggles because I'm out here trying to fight the same battles.

I have my own problems to do deal with.

I'm still picking cotton.

Guilt manifests itself in different ways. For some of us, it's meant that we've made deliberate decisions to be part of the solution. To channel our influence, privilege and power to make a real difference in a way that addresses the root causes of racism and inequity that doesn't rely on prioritising white comfort.

Is this a bit too much for a business book? Well, it depends. We are all human and flawed individuals at that. I am no different.

To process the words written on the preceding pages is to do so with more understanding about how I've had to do the introspection that I'm also asking you to do. We all have work to do; it's just different. And it's so necessary to do this, if we are ever to stand a chance of freeing ourselves from the hundreds of years of insidious conditioning by systemic racism. Make no mistake – it harms white people too, but the impact is acutely felt by Black and other global majority people.

Anti-racism and advancing racial equity are not about revenge. Neither is it about domination, exploitation or being anti-white.

It's not about anti-whiteness, anti-white supremacy, anti-exclusion.

It's about pro fairness, pro equity. It's about redistributing power rather than hoarding it.

What is so divisive about that?

Beyond the Lived Experience

I have almost two decades of HR experience, working for a range of national and international companies, covering everything from risk management to books, fashion to food, telecoms to coffee. But it wasn't my HR experience on its own that got me here, and it certainly didn't happen overnight.

I began recording a video a day for one hundred consecutive days, talking about my experiences but also offering words of advice, encouragement and challenge to decision makers. I did not expect my soft-focus pixelated videos to gather momentum, but they did. Soon after, I was featured in *Forbes*, became one of LinkedIn's Top Voices for 2020 and won HR Most Influential Thinker 2021, awarded by a top UK HR publication. Considering that I speak about racism pretty much every day, these are a few of the 'trophies' I'm happy to display with pride. Along with that came the comments. The emails. The voice notes. Phone calls, tweets, DMs.

From CEOs, founders, investors, diversity and inclusion leads, chief people officers and colleagues who realised their organizations had a problem, or in some cases problems, plural. CEOs realised their companies were 'too white' and 'too homogeneous'. The 'About Us' page on their websites suddenly became a focal point of conversation.

Diversity and inclusion leads quietly admitted that even under the banner of equity, their initiatives failed to specifically tackle race – not in depth and certainly not in a way that gave them any confidence their workplace cultures were genuinely welcoming of all colleagues.

Chief people officers didn't know how to lead the change and were either pressured to do something, fast(!), or encouraged to do nothing and 'wait for the storm to pass'.

Investors responded to consumer pressure and public opinion and turned their focus to all white boards, citing governance risks due to a lack of diversity and social risks due to a failure to address social justice issues that have a material impact on people and communities.

Colleagues became vocal activists, collectively coming together across different ethnicities not only to demand change, but to hold leadership teams accountable for 'walking the talk' and addressing racial discrimination and harassment that was the unchallenged elephant in the room.

A moment in time on 25 May 2020 had changed everything.

This book is an opportunity. No matter how much I may make you wince with my uncompromising honesty in what needs to change and how, it is an opportunity for you to stay with me. But it is also a chance for you to be a role model of moral courage, because in order to go back to your company and ask your colleagues to scrutinise their relationship with racism, you have to be willing to do the same. And I would not ask you to do this, unless I too was doing the work.

Whilst at this stage you might feel tempted to close the book and pick it up again another day when you're more 'in the mood', all I require of you is to stay curious – curious enough to want to know more, to think creatively, to question workplace behaviours, systems and practices that until this point probably seemed normal, perhaps even natural.

Back to the point about writing a book that gives you all the answers: This isn't one of those.

Instead, I offer you a framework, based on thousands of conversations, of the transformative work I have spearheaded as part of leading my advisory firm, HR rewired. The information in this book utilises the experience I have in the challenges and immense opportunities open to us all when we embrace a growth mindset and remain open to new information, new experiences and new perspectives. Where appropriate, I'll share resources with you, places you can go for further insight, yet mostly I'm asking you to do the majority of the work.

Whilst there is only so much one book can cover, you can visit Shereen-daniels.com for further resources and guidance that align with the key themes we are about to explore.

I am a firm believer in co-creation. Rather than tell you what to do, I will provide a foundation for you to explore and ask better questions, because only you can decide what being an anti-racist organization looks and feels like.

Thus the way you apply the principles and perspectives outlined in this book will be based on several concepts:

- How you define what your version of great looks like
- How honest you are willing to be with yourself and your teams about the journey ahead
- How committed you are to move beyond the temptation to focus on 'low-hanging fruit' and instead prioritise and invest in programmes that make a difference for those most impacted
- How willing you are to confront systemic racism and discrimination within your organization and your wider ecosystem
- How comfortable you are to prioritise colleagues, suppliers, partners and other stakeholders who don't look like you.

Throughout each of the chapters you will also come across quotes, from an array of directors, leaders, DEI and HR leads who also struggled at times with their ignorance, discomfort and, in some cases, resentment about why this issue was now on their agenda. Perhaps their positioning is similar to yours, or to that of your colleagues or peers, and if so, that is something to reflect on.

Who Is This Book For?

A safe answer would be to say 'everyone'. Everyone who cares, who wants to make a difference and be part of the solution. But as you'll come to realise, I'm direct and I like specifics. Because it means there is no room for misunderstanding, and we don't waste time and energy on things that make very little substantive difference to the issue at hand.

You have organizations to run. People to lead. Customers to engage and delight. Shareholders to keep happy. Communities to serve. And amongst all of that, a life to lead with people you hold dear. Time is precious. We don't have a lot of it and what we do have has to be used effectively.

The Anti-Racist Organization: Dismantling Systemic Racism in the Workplace is a book for leaders. Particularly white leaders, who occupy the majority of executive positions in corporations on both sides of the Atlantic. Those of you who:

- Suddenly found yourselves having to speak with confidence and clarity about an issue that you may have avoided talking about, both personally and professionally
- Want to exercise your power, privilege and influence to exact change for groups of colleagues, who to varying degrees have been consistently silenced, marginalised and excluded from opportunities because of their ethnicity
- Care about social justice and want to ensure that actions and interventions make a difference in a way that goes beyond ticking boxes

- Want to align anti-racism to your core values and business objectives in a way that is meaningful and not performative or tokenistic
- Have the ability to put your head above the parapet, to ask tough questions of yourself and others, and be prepared to listen, really listen, and have your views, beliefs and perspectives of the world challenged
- Are willing to work hard to resist feeling superior, of being the saviour, of taking action geared towards what looks good rather than what makes a difference and when times get tough, doesn't resort to "can't do right for doing wrong" thinking.

An End to Business Cases?

The business case for dismantling systemic racism is not one of economics. Many people have suggested I talk more about the financial benefits that come with addressing this, yet I don't need to, partly because there are plenty of studies and articles totaling how much exclusion costs our economies, but more importantly because I'm not about to build a business case to address inequality or basic human rights.

Instead, this book is an opportunity for those who want to hear from someone who has publicly and privately committed, day in and day out, to doing the work to unlock thousands of global conversations about race. Who has been doing the work with brands and organizations all over the world who decided they could no longer do nothing. Partnering with leaders who wanted to build deeper partnerships with their colleagues, customers and communities who wanted to evolve their cultures to become more anti-racist, equitable and kind and who every day practice pushing past their discomfort and defensiveness about racism to understand the interconnectedness of all of our experiences, recognising it's impossible to separate what happens in society from what plays out within the four walls of their companies. And that the root causes of what negatively impacts one community damages us all.

This book is about recognising the cost of silence, of looking the other way, of doing little to nothing about an issue that was raised to the forefront of society (again) by the murder of George Floyd on 25 May 2020, which we all saw on our television screens and mobile phones.

This book is about acknowledging that your colleagues are human beings first, and that prioritising the needs of Black people – whether they are friends, family members, peers, colleagues, customers, suppliers, partners or community members – is nothing to be afraid or ashamed of.

This book is about understanding what it takes to be an anti-racist organization and genuinely dismantle systemic racism within your workplace.

The work is done when we no longer need to use the word 'anti-racist'.

Entering the Global Race for Racial Equality

The company was not as far ahead as we should have been.
I wasn't as far ahead as I should be.
I felt exposed as a leader, and as an organization because we didn't have our shit together, and the issues of systemic racism affect our colleagues. Therefore it affected me. And I felt it should affect us all.
Client, 2020

Can you remember a time in your career where you thought there would be so many conversations happening about race? And did you ever, for a second, foresee that you would have to spearhead some of these conversations and lead those actions?

Times have truly changed, yet not everyone has bought into the evolved expectation of what it takes to be a responsible and sustainable company.

When the murder of George Floyd occurred, the resulting global protests were on a scale we'd never seen before. George Floyd wasn't the first and we have a way to go before we can confidently say he is the last, but in that moment of time, everything in society changed, and organizations were not exempt.

> *What are we doing to address this? Are we doing enough? I don't even know where to begin with this.*
> Chief Executive Officer, 2020

'Stakeholder capitalism' has increasingly become a common way to describe the expectation that companies provide long-term value creation. Going beyond a binary focus on shareholder returns, it's now encompassing customers,

Centring profit	Centring people
We focus predominantly on ensuring shareholder value. The way we talk, operate and communicate externally is driven by maximising shareholder returns and is dominated by a profit-and-loss mentality.	We focus predominantly on ensuring stakeholder value and delivering through responsible business practices. The way we talk, operate and communicate externally is driven by recognising the needs of all our stakeholders and by factoring that into our decision-making.

Figure 1.1   Stakeholder capitalism spectrum.
Source: © HR rewired

suppliers, colleagues, investors, communities and others who have a stake in the business, generating value for all stakeholders, not just for shareholders.

Where does your organization sit?

It is not as simple as the assumption that you are either for or against stakeholder capitalism, that you are either a capitalist or an anti-capitalist. It's more nuanced than that. Instead, think of it as a spectrum. At one end of the scale, customers, employees and communities are merely tools to maximise profits for the benefit of shareholders. At the opposite end, companies exist for the benefit of the public good: purpose beyond profit, and ensuring the needs of as many stakeholders as possible are met.

You have a choice in deciding where you fit on that spectrum and much of that will be driven by your values, your mission and how you want to be perceived in your industry and by the world at large.

Stakeholder capitalism is not a new term – in fact, it goes back to the Great Depression – but it has a new relevance. Dozens of the world's largest companies, representing trillions of pounds in market capitalization, have pledged to use a uniform set of "Stakeholder Capitalism Metrics" as part of the mainstream disclosures. This was announced 26 January 2021 by the World Economic Forum and its International Business Council when leaders from governments and corporates convened for a virtual version of the annual Davos conference. These commitments were seen as an opportunity to address the Sustainable Development Goals (SDGs; also known as Global Goals), adopted by the United Nations in 2015 as a universal call to action to end poverty, protect the planet and ensure that by 2030 all people would enjoy peace and prosperity.

Regardless of whether you are a fan or a critic of environmental, social and governance (ESG) standards and to what extent you believe they are a legitimate tool to drive more sustainable and responsible business practices, it isn't possible to operate in today's and tomorrow's environment without an awareness of how your company operates against these standards.

The leadership teams with an edge on adjusting their approach to delivering against new expectations in tackling racism are those who are using this movement to redefine their values and purpose to ensure there is an alignment between their words and actions. On the flip side, stakeholders are continually looking for indicators that reinforce commitments.

Stakeholder capitalism isn't without its critics, of course. It's easy to claim you are a people-centered company and give the illusion of caring about your stakeholders, even if your day-to-day culture and practices tell a different story.

The reality is that in the minds of some leaders, maximising profit means avoiding anything controversial that may damage public perception, which in turn hits the bottom line.

What is controversial?

Racism.

Whether we care to admit it – irrespective of how much quantitative and qualitative data exists to show that modern society still has an issue with racism, that everyday human rights are being violated and often recorded on mobile phones and talked about in real time on social media – for some, genuinely addressing the issue is too risky.

Silence on issues relating to racism was the smart and safe play. Until silence itself become controversial.

We saw a plethora of companies change their social media feeds to black, and incorporate the latest trending

Black Lives Matter hashtag to ensure they were seen to be acting in solidarity with the Black community. Whilst the world was distracted, there wasn't an initial focus on the substance of these commitments. The hype was real, and well-known brands swiftly committed to doubling or tripling the number of Black hires in senior positions (conveniently using percentage language, which doesn't sound nearly as great when you realise that doubling the percentage of Black managers by 50% actually means hiring one more Black person if there's only currently one Black person on the board), and propelled ever-increasing budgets to social justice funds like auctioneers at *Homes Under the Hammer*. Anecdotal stories abound of companies committing millions in social justice funding, only to have it revealed that a year later barely a penny had been spent. It quickly became apparent that a lot of organizations opted for style over substance.

This sudden pressure to act caught many unawares. In their bid to do something, many took knee-jerk and fragmented actions, sometimes simply rehashing old approaches to diversity and inclusion and relabelling them as anti-racism.

Because who were you if you weren't anti-racist?

Racial equity as a term came later. When there was a concern the word racism was too divisive.

However, the general public and colleagues wised up and began to scrutinise who was doing what and what was their quantifying impact.

Statements, hashtags, clever social media posts were no longer cutting it. Companies had to do something, so where did the majority start?

> *We are revamping our policies and reaching out to our Black colleagues. They are in so much pain and it breaks my heart.*
> HR manager, 2020

Developing Awareness

The most typical response to addressing racism is found in the belief that policies, procedures and HR technology (bizarrely) are the holy grail of where racism lives and dies. It's the default action when it becomes apparent that there is an issue with how certain groups are treated, and it becomes the go-to item on the job description for new diversity, equity and inclusion hires.

Not enough Black candidates? Buy a tech solution that promises to eliminate bias. Lack of representation at board level? Brief the executive search company to 'get more, and fast'. Complaints about racial discrimination and harassment? Update your policy and emphasise that you take a zero-tolerance approach to racism. Even better, run a survey and ask colleagues how many times they've witnessed racism.

These are the default actions when it becomes apparent there are issues with how certain groups are treated, and they become the go-to items on the job description for new diversity, equity and inclusion hires.

That is absolutely part of what you may need to look at it, but it isn't the whole picture. These approaches lack context, depth and nuance, and offer little to no evaluation of root causes.

There is likely a recognition that your processes, policies, systems – the informal and formal ways of doing things – may not be as inclusive as they should be. But there may also be a recognition that your company perpetuates racism. Not because you hire bad people or because you've deliberately set out to oppress certain groups. But if you don't confront the roots of what excludes people due to their ethnicity, if you fail to challenge your own preconceptions of what racism is and what it isn't, and if you use your discomfort as a convenient barrier to block change, this is exactly how we've gotten here today. In what's meant to be the most technologically advanced period known to humankind, our apathy, discomfort and fear allow the system called racism – because that's what it is, a system – to continue doing its best work. It is a system that perpetuates consistent favourable outcomes for some and consistent unfavourable outcomes for others, a system that isn't confined just to the US, despite what we believe in the UK; neither is it a nonissue in predominantly Black or Brown countries.

Ignorance is bliss when racism doesn't impact you. But in a post-2020 world, ignorance isn't so blissful when you are expected to disclose why you have taken little to no meaningful action to diversify your business, and to take the necessary steps to root out discrimination and inequity and address the issues in a sustainable way.

Forget the panic and emotion we see orchestrated by the media. Think about the questions you are being asked at board meetings, town halls, earnings calls. The information you are expected to share in your annual reports, disclosures and the like. It's changed, hasn't it? It will continue to change. One could predict that there will be even more support for shareholder proposals that specifically address climate and social issues, and rather than being separate, governance is woven in.

There is already a much greater weight put on how your business operations impact the welfare of all your stakeholders, not just the ones you deem 'valuable'. There is a disruption to the notion of assigning value to what works for the majority. Even the idea that you can't please everyone is geared towards majority rules.

Who are the majority within your organization? Where do they sit within your hierarchy? How much influence do they have? Are they the ones who influence your decisions about not only what you do, but the depths, the commitment and the speed of action?

Is their discomfort central to your decision-making?

In their 2021 report 'The Economic State of Black America', consulting firm McKinsey & Company identified that it would take 95 years for Black workers to reach talent parity with their white counterparts. Their research analysed overall employment data from 24 companies, including some of the largest private-sector employers in the United States, who participated in this research across a total of about 3.7 million US employees. Some other key statistics include:

- Black employees are underrepresented in the highest-growth geographies and the highest-paid industries.
- Black employees are overrepresented in low-growth geographies and in frontline jobs, which tend to pay less.
- In the private sector, 45% of Black employees (6.7 million people) work in three industries that have a large frontline-service presence: healthcare, retail and accommodation and food service.
- Black employees are underrepresented in IT, professional services and financial services.
- Black private-sector workers, 43%, make less than $30,000 per year, compared with 29% of the rest of private-sector employees.
- Black workers believe their organizations are less fair, accepting and authentic.

- Black workers face greater hurdles to gainful employment than do the rest of the labor force, creating stark disparities. For example, the employment rates for Black workers with some college or an associate's degree are similar to the total population of workers who have a high school diploma.
  McKinsey & Company, 2021

Between October and December 2020 in the UK, the unemployment rate rose from 24.5% to 41.6% for Black people aged 16–24, three times more than white workers of the same age, where it rose from 10.1% to 12.4% (Office for National Statistics, 2021).

In August 2021, the US Bureau of Labor Statistics disclosed that the Black unemployment rate went up from 8.2% to 8.8%. In comparison, the white unemployment rate dropped by 0.3% to 4.5%; the Asian unemployment rate dropped 0.7% to 4.6%; and the unemployment rate for Hispanic and Latino workers fell 0.2% to 6.4%. Black unemployment is almost 50% higher than white unemployment levels (US Bureau of Labor Statistics, 2021).

The Start of Uncomfortable Questions

How do you establish impactful programmes that not only dismantle systemic racism but also set a strong foundation for a sustainable business that sees the social and governance aspects of ESG frameworks and stakeholder capitalism as an opportunity to do more and to do better, not to get away with doing the bare minimum through force and compliance? And here are some more things to consider:

- How do you ease the friction between competing stake-holder interests?
- What is the impact on the decisions you make about allocating capital and resources?
- How do you think about risk (political, public perception, colleague expectation and changes to customer attitudes)?
- How confident are you in the leadership capability of your teams to play their part in dismantling systemic racism? Or is there a nagging thought that they might be part of the problem?

Managing talent is probably one of the top priorities for executive boards around the globe. How do you motivate, inspire and unleash the potential of colleagues who are essential for where you are headed? Colleagues who get your mission, whose behaviour aligns with your values and who already have put their hat in the ring to help transform your culture for the benefit of everyone?

What is your course of action for those who prefer that things stay the way they are, silent or not so silent saboteurs who are resistant to change?

How do you navigate changing societal expectations? Macro issues are now having a direct impact on strategy and execution. What were once abstract theories for once-a-year conferences are now monthly if not weekly conversations with no one person having all the answers.

It's a lot, isn't it?

We've moved on from being able to get away with vague platitudes and sound bites that look good in a social media post or as a quote in your diversity and inclusion report – despite the fact this is still extremely commonplace.

We cannot return to business as usual if we are unable to grapple with an issue that affects individuals on a global scale.

Even if you believe it's political correctness gone mad, this is the new expectation. Therefore, this is the time to be honest and recognise that while you may not have all the answers and you're still unsure about what steps to take, you need to move away from the preconceived ideas about what racism is and why it's still an issue.

This is where the skills of unlearning and relearning come in, because instead, you need to reverse engineer your approach and seek to change the conditions, your workplace cultures and behaviours so that it works for everyone, not just the 'majority' who look like you. Lean into that discomfort; it's a sign of growth. Demonstrate moral courage and be willing to take the lead, rather than seeking safety through consensus. And do it in a way where there is a depth to the work, giving you a prime opportunity to put in solid foundations to increase equity, inclusion and safety for all of your colleagues, without having to keep repeating the same change programmes over and over again.

Your customers, colleagues, investors and key shareholders want to see you committing to and delivering on action. This is the time to be honest and recognise that while you may not have all the answers and you're not sure what steps to take, it's time to move away from the expectation of fixing people. Instead, you need to reverse-engineer your approach and seek to change the conditions in your workplace culture so that it works for everyone, not just the 'majority' who look like you.

Having conversations internally is important, but they must go somewhere. Every organization that has knocked on my door since the summer of 2020 has had the same problem, no matter who they are. Multinationals, growing startups, household names and brands across a dizzying array of industries all explain to me, in almost the exact same way, 'Shereen, we want to do something, but we don't know what or how or even where to begin.'

They're convinced they've been too slow to act. They're worried about answering questions, about why it's taken them so long. They are different from the companies I've previously mentioned, whose social media teams are keen to show action through the liberal use of trending hashtags.

These executive leaders made the decision to do something, but despite an unwavering commitment, they're nervous. For many it's uncharted territory; they didn't want to be the first, yet they don't want to be last. They're fearful that their lack of action will reflect badly on their organization. They don't want to get it wrong but they aren't sure they 100% want to get it right. They don't want to spend too much money. They're apprehensive about taking things too far. And they believe they must avoid the 'politics' of race and are desperate to find a way to do something that's safe and won't upset their white colleagues under the guise of ensuring that they're 'on everyone's on side'.

In their own words, here's a snippet of what they were grappling with:

- We're a majority white, male and middle-aged board. None of us have a clue where to start.
- Watching your videos has made me realise we don't really understand as much as we thought we did.
- I don't have access to anyone credible whom we trust to help us navigate this area. Lots of diversity and inclusion

consultants out there claim they can help, but how do we know who to choose?

- I know representation is an issue. It's embarrassing and I want to fix it, but suddenly just hiring more Black people doesn't feel right. Or is that what we should focus on?

- My HR team is majority white; that's also an issue, isn't it?

- We've never trained our managers on anything to do with race and racism. In fact, we've barely talked about it as a business, and I don't know where we should start.

- If people make mistakes, they're only human, but should we just fire them? Is that what we should be doing now?

- We understand our approach needs to be aligned to our business strategy, but how do we do that?

- What do we call you people? Can we say Black?

- Should we be talking about this in our other territories? How do we do that? I'm particularly thinking about Africa – there isn't racism over there like there is here, is there? So maybe this isn't relevant for them?

- I'm being asked more challenging questions by our shareholders and if I'm honest, I don't feel confident and comfortable with my answers.

- We don't really have a budget for this, but we know we need to do something. What can you suggest?

- We've done a lot, but we feel like we are a seven out of ten. How do we get to ten? How do I know that we're doing enough?

- We've spent a lot of time on listening and raising awareness. How do we convert it to action?

- Our Black colleagues are reluctant to come back to the office after extended periods working from home and/or they are still leaving, despite everything we've done. What are we doing wrong?

- Does it matter that I'm the only person leading this, that I'm the only person who cares?
- Not everyone is supportive of what we're trying to do. How do we deal with that?
- What about everyone else?

Does any of this sound familiar? And in reading this list, think about whether you noticed these things missing:

- No mention of how their Black colleagues or customers were thinking or feeling
- No mention of what it was like to live, work and play in a society that was accepting of racial inequities and inequalities
- Little recognition of the inherent power and privilege afforded to leaders who could objectively debate and discuss a course of action according to convenience, comfort, ease and 'affordability'
- Very few questions about how to ensure their products and services don't perpetuate harm
- Some (not all) mentioned how the lack of substantive action is impacting their Black colleagues, but even when they did it was to express sympathy (tinged with pity) rather than compassion (empathy tied to action).

That's why so many, to this day, struggle to take the necessary steps to address systemic racism within their corporate structures. I say this not to judge but to highlight the reality of what sits beneath public pledges of solidarity and commitment to change, and what our reluctance to tackle this has led to. Logically, we know that systemic racism is a bad thing, that it's unfair and we should all do better, but practically, it feels uncomfortable and messy. Plus, isn't it a problem for society to fix, not an agenda item for the boardroom?

Public perception matters – sometimes more than the impact on the colleagues most impacted.

A Day That Changed Everything

Everyone assumed that the death of George Floyd officially started the global race to equality, with everyone else coming out of the gates hard and fast. But that wasn't the case.

Yes, some did, for a variety of reasons – some personal, some not. Yet it actually serves no purpose to ruminate on this in an attempt to explain away the delay in taking action, other than seeking reassurance that other companies are lagging too.

The other point to note is that even though some companies did start their journey earlier, that doesn't necessarily mean they're ahead of the curve. Speed doesn't equate to depth of understanding and quality of action. Thoughtful action is better than knee-jerk statements and aspirational goals that sound good but don't actually effect change in the long run.

Think about where your company was in the summer of 2020. What actions did you take? How much time, money and resources have you dedicated to this so far? To what extent has it made a difference? How would your Black colleagues respond to these questions?

Think about where your company is today. How much has changed? What are some of the conversations you're having now? Where are the challenges? What is stopping you from realising your ambitions to be seen as a company that is taking this seriously?

Whilst timing or speed doesn't necessarily equate to a better outcome, by the same token, claiming you are too busy or there is too much activity in your corporate calendar to give this the attention it needs is a delaying tactic your colleagues and stakeholders can see through. If people and culture are the bedrock of your company, then anything detrimental to the psychological and physical safety of your workforce needs to be addressed and prioritised.

Doesn't it?

> *We really want to do something about this, but my organization is not quite ready. I need to do more to convince them. I'm embarrassed to say it, but I'm being honest. This is what I'm dealing with.*
> Global chief diversity and inclusion officer, 2021

So in this case, timing doesn't necessarily equate to a better outcome. Yet by the same token, claiming you are too busy or there is too much activity in your corporate calendar to give this the attention it needs is a delay tactic your colleagues and shareholders can see right through.

Like most things in business, it's not always about what you did or didn't do. It's the why behind it that makes all the difference.

Whether you did a little bit of something or a whole lot of nothing, can you articulate why that was? Does your reason sound plausible? And if you had your time again, would you have done the same thing?

> *It suddenly struck me just how white my leadership board is. I'm embarrassed to say this but I never really noticed it before.*
> Founder and CEO, 2021

How Tokenism Became the Answer

It's the ultimate elephant in the room, isn't it? Despite decades of proclamations of diversity and inclusion, boardrooms have basically remained the same.

You might not have noticed, but others certainly did. Your colleagues would have noticed, and your shareholders too. Not everyone would have cared, of course, but it would have been noted.

In years gone by, it was enough simply to talk about diversity and inclusion initiatives, and to proclaim commitment to encouraging everyone to be themselves, to accept people for who they are and what they bring to the table. Authenticity was a key word, used repeatedly, a badge of honour to ensure that talented colleagues felt like they belonged. Yet despite this emphasis on recognising and valuing difference, corporate boards remained mysteriously the same. And in fact, it was seen as a 'positive' to have a majority white cisgendered male board, one gleaned from a specific socioeconomic background.

Homogeny was dressed up as culture fit.

But not now. All those perceived positives have suddenly shifted to become negatives. And they're not just negatives for large conglomerates or listed corporations. These factors affect small operations too, because as long as you have colleagues, investors and clients, specifics will now be asked of you. In order to succeed in the post-2020 world, your company will need to get really comfortable about answering the tough questions about the climate crisis, gender and now race and ethnicity.

If you're reading this believing that you've made real inroads into tackling systemic racism within your company,

I promise you there is still value in reading this book. Consider it this way: How confident are you in your ability to demonstrate credible action plans rooted in clearly defined problem statements, which themselves are based on the right quantitative and qualitative data sources and where your impact centres those most affected by racism?

Consider these scenarios:

- If an investor was ready to invest £100 million into your company on the proviso that you could detail the specific actions you've taken to address systemic racism within your workplace, how confident are you that you would get the full £100 million?
- If a regulatory body was reviewing your licence to operate in new territories or markets, on the proviso that you could detail the specific actions you've taken to address systemic racism within your workplace and extending to the products and services you offer, how confident would you be that your licence would be granted?
- If your government was about to award continued funding to enable you to serve the general public, on the proviso that you could show how you understand the interconnected elements of how race, gender and social class contribute to exclusion and marginalization within your workplace and the communities you serve, and demonstrate the steps you've taken to address that, would you still get the funding?
- How would you score if your entire workforce was to conduct an appraisal of how you've performed? Part of the evaluation criteria would look at:

- The extent to which your leadership and managerial teams understand the context of racism and their role in being part of the solution
- How far you have listened to Black colleagues and regularly solicited feedback on initiatives and programs
- Holding leadership teams to account, including tackling individuals whose behaviour consistently does not align with professed statements and commitments
- Evaluating the formal and informal ways decisions are made to ensure there is representation, that the loudest, most senior, and most privileged voices are not always the ones that are prioritised
- How safe colleagues feel to raise issues and feel confident that you will do something about it, without scapegoating, tone policing or gaslighting
- How far you've delivered on public pledges to do better and do more
- Whether everyone understands that equity isn't reverse racism or discrimination in disguise

Questions like these go beyond equality initiatives and the blanket solution of hiring more Black executives. Instead, they query the culture inherent in your company. Challenge your judgement: How is it you never saw that your board and senior leadership teams consistently remained so white? And question the actions behind your publicised commitments to change.

It isn't about rolling out the blanket statement of 'we are still on a journey'. Yet conversely, it's not about perfection either. Instead, it's demonstrating that you have done the work to at least ensure there is clarity about the root causes of the issues, not just the symptoms. That you're designing considered and intentional action plans and executing with the right metrics that extends right through your ecosystem. Rather than doggedly holding tight to something just so you can tick it off your to-do list, you're experimenting and course-correcting based on continuous feedback.

Until the summer of 2020, racial tokenism was a societally accepted form of 'solving the race issue' and was considered sufficient for bettering equality and being seen to do the right thing.

But that was all it was: 'being seen'.

That's okay, we'll just hire more Black people.
Chairperson, 2021

Tokenism was accepted because race is so visual. You can appear to be doing something by, for example, putting a smiling Black woman on the cover of your annual report or promoting a Black man to senior management. Even better if they are Black, have a visible disability, look gender fluid and their sexual identification is open for debate.

Brilliant. Killing two birds with one stone. Let's have some of that. The job is done. Mission accomplished; you now have a diverse team.

But it is pretence. It's too easy. And it's lazy.

When we asked about the single most important attribute being prioritised in the board's next director search, racial/ethnic diversity topped the list (25%). It ranked higher than traditional areas like industry expertise (20%) and operational expertise (14%). Gender diversity ranked much lower, at 12%, perhaps because boards have done a lot of work to bring on female directors in the past few years – if only one or two.
PWC Corporate Directors Survey, 2021 (pwc.com)

Due to the ease of visual representation, for years we've ended up with these surface-level gestures of racial equity and after the summer of 2020, we just amped it up a bit more. Note also that the term 'racial equity' came later, amid concern that the word 'racism' was too divisive.

That approach of doing of something merely to garner output is no longer enough. The representational box-ticking exercise of 'how many Black people are on your board' doesn't cut it anymore. It's tokenistic, transactional and non-transformative. It advances absolutely nothing.

Therein lies the difference between tokenism and representation. Representation is important. In context.

You should be asking why it is seemingly impossible for anyone who does not look like the majority of your colleagues to progress above first- or second-line management positions.

- Why are there few or no Black leaders on your board?
- Why are you so keen on emphasising proportional representation?
- What are the retention and promotion rates for Black colleagues?
- What are they paid, relative to their white counterparts?
- Who is asking those questions to your line managers, heads of department and functional directors?
- Who rubber-stamps the answers? Someone must do, if very little has changed.

What you do with the answers to these questions will determine how serious you are about dismantling systemic racism within your workplace.

Suddenly promoting or hiring more Black people is not the answer. There's more to it than that.

References

McKinsey & Company. (17 June 2021). The Economic State of Black America. Retrieved 14 September 2021, from https://www.mckinsey.com/featured-insights/diversity-and-inclusion/the-economic-state-of-black-america-what-is-and-what-could-be.

Office for National Statistics. (December 2021). Labour market overview, UK. Retrieved 14 September 2021, from https://www.ons.gov.uk/employmentandlabourmarket/peopleinwork/employmentandemployeetypes/bulletins/uklabourmarket/latest.

PwC's Annual Corporate Directors Survey. (2021). Retrieved 6 January 2022, from https://www.pwc.com/us/en/services/governance-insights-center/library/annual-corporate-directors-survey.html.

US Bureau of Labor Statistics. (2021). Labor Force Statistics from the Current Population Survey. Retrieved 14 September 2021, from https://www.bls.gov/cps/.

Moving Beyond Conversations

It's not my fault.
I didn't invent racism.
I never enslaved Black people.
I don't see colour.
I've only ever hired the best person for the job.

Clients, 2020–2021

We Live in a Racialised Society

We don't understand racism.

Our lack of moral courage in at least talking accurately about racism, whether in the workplace or in the wider society, means that we have reduced it to overt, easily identified behaviour.

Depending on the individual, the position they hold and how valuable they are to the company, we may be unceasing in our vilification of individuals, their specific actions and the agendas we deem racist. But a zero-tolerance approach to racism is never truly zero tolerance. And it can't be, because racism is insidious and isn't just about how we act.

We brush off racism as incidents isolated to specific individuals' opinions and actions, ones we soon forget when the individual is, hopefully, disgraced. Yet when we inevitably push these matters out of our minds, making the conscious decision to 'move on' with the mechanics of our own lives, we completely misconstrue racism's existence.

We deceive ourselves, comfort ourselves even, into believing that these odd, occasional incidents by rash individuals are racism in its entirety – something wholly separate from us and from the values on which we base our lives. When we do this we trivialise racism's reality.

> *I do not condone racism, under any circumstances.*
> *This behaviour is abhorrent to me.*
> *I would never hire anyone who I thought was racist.*
> *Not all white people are racist.*
>
> Clients, 2020

> *I was really offended. I'm a nice person. I don't have a racist bone in my body.*
>
> HR consultant, 2020

We may focus more on whether we are being accused of something, hoping to hear, 'Oh, I don't mean you of course', which we can take to mean that we are somehow separate from the issue. If it's not us, we can continue to talk about those 'bad people' over there.

We subconsciously dismiss racism's origin story, where it came from and how, all these centuries later, it's still here. It continues to do its work, barely interrupted, despite the technological advances and the claims that we are a more enlightened and civilised society.

Racism is so entrenched within the fabric of our society that we can't imagine living any other way. And whether or not we want to address it consciously, we do live in a racialised society.

But the concept of race doesn't actually exist. It was fabricated to serve a specific purpose that dates back to the seventeenth century, when philosophers were engaging in their own version of blue-sky thinking and designing what they thought would be the ideal society for men like them to get and stay ahead.

Simply put, the founding principles upon which Western society is built purposefully created the racist ideology we live by. And make no mistake – we do live by it. We may not have been around when its concrete foundations were poured, but we exist in the structures those foundations support. We've never questioned the inherent fairness of those structures, because it works, for the majority at least. And is it our responsibility to fix something we never had a hand in creating?

Racism is one of the best manmade systems every created. Over five hundred years later it is still doing exactly what it was designed to do. And it feeds off our apathy, compliance and obedience. It rewards insecurity, superiority and scarcity.

Despite how uncomfortable this makes you feel, we do live in a society that values whiteness. This creates and reinforces power structures that work for the benefit of white people – to different degrees, of course, but whiteness is central to pretty much everything, with the intended consequence being that Black people (at least in Western society) exist with little or no institutional power to improve our situation. We are not represented en masse in the political and corporate corridors of power. We are punished rather than rewarded for doing anything that seeks to improve the experiences of people who look like us. In some cases this is referred to as reverse racism and is actively discouraged, lest we be accused of favouring our own.

There might be one or two of us, of course, who have somehow got to that magical seat at the table, but as we've seen time and again, the conscious and subconscious limiting of Black representation doesn't just pose a challenge for the 'About Us' section of corporate websites.

We aren't here protesting, calling for and instigating change because we don't have the will or the capability. It's because the systems and structures we inhabit are deliberately not skewed in our favour.

Decisions that affect Black colleagues are universally made by white people. Even if you claim to consult, fundamentally you have the final call. Despite our objections, we don't have the power, rank or privilege to influence those decisions – not really, despite proclamations to the contrary.

We have an open-door policy and we listen to our colleagues. Those issues are in society. We definitely don't have any of that here.
CEO, 2021

You might be thinking, why keep bringing up this messy, complex societal issue and making it a corporate problem? Why can't we keep it separate? It's too emotional, too divisive and now if you say the wrong thing you're done for.

There is no space for 'politics' within the workplace.

In order to advance racial equity within your organization, you need to understand how we arrived at this point in the first place. We got here through rational thinking, through logic and objectivity as decided centuries ago by white Englishmen.

In a strange way, we got there through politics, as defined as the activities associated with the governance of a country or area, especially the debate between parties having power.

The Age of Enlightenment

Common cultural sense hasn't really changed since the seventeenth century, when politically active English philosophers, white men like Thomas Hobbes and John Locke, argued that religious-based hostilities within England were holding the nation back from global supremacy.

They argued for a capitalist England, one that in order to reach its full potential would require reshaping along the lines of reason rather than religion. The national project would necessitate the input of rational men. This is what would be needed to steer the country to further prosperity. And when a bunch of self-serving, wealthy seventeenth-century white men got together to chat about what rational looked like, they came up with an image of themselves.

There's nothing inherently wrong with that. The problem was that their view of the world became the prevailing view of the world.

Logic.

Reason.

Supremacy.

So during this Enlightened era, if you weren't a white wealthy man, by default you were deemed irrational. And to be less than rational was to be less than human, because it wasn't long before 'rational' became the gold standard of humanity.

Such philosophical ideas are illogical but they really mattered, because back in the seventeenth century the philosophers with wealthy connections had political sway. These guys weren't writing manifestos to be read only by a few academics and later to become forgotten dust magnets on library shelves. They were directly influencing global politics: capitalist ideology and individualism in England and France, and foundational politics in America.

So with the preeminent belief that the ideal human was none other than the wealthy white Englishman, it doesn't take much imagination to conclude who stood at the opposite end of the scale and was ranked the least, or even less than human.

The Black man. The Black woman.

And when the white world started seeing Black people as less than human, as the 'savage antithesis' to the rational white man, it changed the way white people thought about justice, about politics and about economics. Who was deemed human and who wasn't became more systemic, codified and regulated so that this tripartite of society, used as a benchmark for humanity, harmonised to cement the newly found concepts of democracy and capitalism with the institution of slavery.

Placing value upon physical differences, such as a skin colour, became the default method of elevating white people and subjugating Black people, so much so that when Thomas Jefferson penned 'all men are created equal. . .with certain unalienable Rights' in the US Declaration of Independence in 1776, he truly meant "all men", because by that time Black people were no longer considered human.

You could say this was a convenient truth for Jefferson because he profited from owning Black humans, but Black people were not excluded solely for Jefferson's personal convenience. By the time the founding fathers of US democracy wrote the Declaration of Independence, the rational, capitalist philosophies of Hobbes and Locke were hardwired into white people's psyches. By this point Hobbes's philosophies had been regarded as truth for nearly a hundred years. His conviction that white people were the most rational of humans because they chose to form 'civilised' societies was already a well-known 'fact', and it rationalised white people's imposition on those Hobbes considered 'savages' (Hobbes, 1651). When John Locke, Jefferson's favourite philosopher, wrote his seminal piece concerning the foundation of human knowledge and understanding (Locke, 1690) nearly a century prior to the Independence pronouncement, his tales of sexual relations between Black women and baboons had already twisted white people's sense of what humanity looked like. He had sown the seed of acceptance that Black people might look human, but that didn't mean they were.

So long before the ink dried on 'all men are created equal', white supremacy was baked into our societal systems. And let's not kid ourselves here; the societal systems we're talking about are those on both sides of the Atlantic.

As the words of these English philosophers became the prevailing discourse supporting the economic and political mastery of wealthy white men, their stories inevitably became the natural order of things across Western societies.

They became normal, the way things are. And therefore, unlike opinions and viewpoints, they were considered value-free and self-evidently correct.

Their words were 'truth'.

They were the lords and masters and it became incumbent on those who were deemed uncivilised to prove their worth and value. This meant being a useful tool for white people to benefit from, not reasserting their humanity.

But let's dial it back a bit. If Black people were nonrational, unequal, exempt from unalienable rights and less than human, then what were we? Where was our place and worth in society?

It was economic. The work of these philosophers of the Enlightenment monetised Black people. They devalued us to an existence of exchangeable units of value, with our worth tied to keeping wealthy, powerful white men, well, wealthy and powerful.

So when governments, brimming with wealthy white men, are more concerned with economic self-preservation, it's no surprise that politics turns away from supporting the common good, and justice becomes a blunt instrument used to enforce and preserve the status quo.

When you think about some of the conversations being had around boardroom tables all over the world, if we're honest, how much has changed since then? Have we really done away with our need to have Black people prove their worth and value to ensure our basic human rights are met? Or are we more enlightened now?

Business cases for diversity and inclusion waxed lyrical about the top-line and bottom-line growth that comes with having 'diverse' teams, rather than recognising exclusion, marginalisation and unfairness. The route to ensure we had equal opportunities, if there is even such a thing, revolved around how profitable it would be.

'It just makes business sense' was the common phrase used. Even in our oppression, we continued to be exploited by white people for commercial gain.

How many tech platforms sprung up off the back of Black Lives Matter, founded by white and other non-Black men (or women)? How many white-led, majority white diversity and inclusion companies were hired to solve this 'Black issue'? Feminists who had spent decades advocating for gender representation and 'forgot' that Black women weren't included suddenly became the go-to experts on how Black women felt and thought.

Opportunistic non-Black businesspeople saw a gap in the market and recognised that whilst they may not be best placed to solve these issues, they were the accepted faces. Easier to get investment, easier to attract nervous brands who felt that solutions from competent Black business owners meant radical programmes or taking things 'too far.'

Engaging with white professionals on this Black issue was a safe and comfortable bet. 'We should do the heavy lifting' was the implicit narrative for white and non-Black people who set up companies to be part of the solution. It's a moral duty. But the heavy lifting was only worthy provided they got paid, running enterprises that often mirrored the same organization dysfunction they offered solutions to.

But who cares, the narrative continued, provided someone offers a solution? Why does skin colour matter here? It just so happens that we prefer to do business with non-Black companies, even if they don't have the expertise. Even if we can't point to anything that makes them credible, that shows they are respected in their field beyond their lived experience. And our Black colleagues would feel comfortable with us using them.

Top executives like to do business with vendors who look like them and understand their world, who 'get' it, people they trust won't take things too far and know the game at play. Expertise and an intimate knowledge of the issue didn't matter; in some cases, is still doesn't.

Black people are an opportunity to make money, whether it's from our joy, our cultures or our trauma. We're fair game and we should be grateful that some action is being taken. It's better than nothing.

This is the ultimate example of benefiting from either outcome when you toss a coin: the privilege of benefiting from our oppression, and the commercial opportunity to be seen as fixing the problem. But this applies only in so far as that it continues to make money, of course. When social justice ceases to hold top- or bottom-line benefits, it will remain to be seen who continues the fight to do the right thing.

Most decision makers don't even give a second thought to the idea that the money they give to suppliers to support them in becoming more equitable actually lines the pockets of the very individuals who have consistently benefited from this racialised society we live in.

If you haven't really thought about it like that, you should. And it will probably make for uncomfortable realisations, at least for some.

I just feel like we are fatigued as an organization. We've been talking about racism for well over a year now. It's all becoming a bit much if I'm honest, and I'm not sure our CEO has the appetite to drive this forward.

People director, 2020

Times have moved on. Yes, laws have changed. We are not physically standing in the plantations anymore. But after generations upon generations of racism being ingrained in *all* of us, updating a law here and there isn't going to change our underlying reality.

Renewing your commitment to diversity and inclusion changes nothing. Engaging with vendors who fail to address the depths and contextual facets of systemic racism is simply putting a plaster on a gaping wound.

Hiring more Black people does something. But it's not the complete picture. Such actions are mere window dressing when the humans underneath are preconditioned differently. When we as a society are inherently racist, surface-level adjustments are about as useful as a chocolate teapot.

Remember, the fate of entire continents was determined by racism, and it continues to this day.

This is merely a glimpse into the depths of racism. There are other books and incredibly insightful authors who dig into the roots of race, and if anything I've written here has piqued your curiosity, I urge you to explore that. Keep an open mind. Don't try and retrofit information to align with your views of the world. This is part of your journey.

It's still part of mine.

I have a lot of conversations with CEOs and HR leaders who say, 'I'd love to advance racial equity in our firm, I really would, but the board would never sign off on something focusing solely on Black people. So can we do something for Black colleagues but also for everybody else, because we don't want to leave people out'.
And therein lies the issue.
We still can't seem to get away from our inherent reluctance to focus on the people most impacted by racism.
It feels unfair.

Shereen Daniels

Wasn't Diversity and Inclusion Supposed to Solve This?

In December 2020 I updated my LinkedIn profile. It was there that I first stated that I'm not about diversity, inclusion or belonging. I was always asked during interviews, 'Are you just saying that to be controversial?' And my answer was always short and sweet.

Traditional diversity and inclusion (D&I) does not work:

Not to fix racism

Not to get to the roots of white supremacy and challenge power structures to create fairer and equitable workplace cultures

Not to provide genuine psychological safety for colleagues to speak out about their experiences and why they feel they are victims of racism, discrimination, harassment, bullying and retaliation

Not when there's a culture of protecting the majority at the expense of the minority

Not when there are still few to no Black people on executive boards

Not when the discomfort about race stops leaders from taking action, because to get involved feels too risky.

> *It was a challenging one for us to deal with. The director concerned was having a bad day and didn't mean it. He even mentors young Black students at his local college so I know for a fact he doesn't have an issue with Black people.*
> HR manager, 2021

> *We're really committed to doing something meaningful. We're just delaying it as we've got some mission-critical projects to land first. Can we come back to you in six months' time and revisit?*
> Global diversity, equity and inclusion lead, 2020

Five hundred years later, we're having the same conversations, hearing the same excuses:

The denial
The apathy
The discomfort
The fear

Nobody ever told me there was a problem. We have Black colleagues in multiple different countries and I've never heard anything to suggest racism is a problem in our company.
                                          Founder and CEO, 2021

Corporate America spends over $8 billion on diversity training each year (Newkirk, 2019). Training people about unconscious bias became the default action to promote diversity and inclusion. Yet hundreds of studies, dating back to the 1930s, state that unconscious bias training does not reduce bias, alter behaviour or change workplaces.

We would love to do more but we've already committed our budget to unconscious bias training, so that's it for this year.
                                          HR director, 2020

It's like Einstein's definition of insanity: doing the same thing repeatedly and expecting different results.

But are we expecting different results? And if we're really honest, how much did we really care about whether the very initiatives we were espousing did anything to address one of the biggest stains on society's soul?

Before you opened this book, you knew traditional diversity programmes didn't make a real difference, because even though your organization has ongoing commitments to D&I training, your workplace demographic does not reflect the population demographic outside its front door.

You already suspected that what you were currently doing doesn't really work, but to call it out and question it would look like you're not supporting the premise of D&I. So instead you said nothing (publicly), shrank the budgets and didn't sign off on recruiting additional resources.

> *We've done a lot of work in this space already. I think it's important we don't forget the difference we've already made and celebrate those wins.*
>
> Managing director, 2021

In 2022, if your company is based in London, nearly 50% of your workforce should be from minoritised communities, because these communities make up approximately 50% of London's population. If this figure is not reflected in your workforce across the company's internal structure from the C-suite down, and there is traditional D&I training in place, something isn't right.

You can't just tweak your current diversity and inclusion initiatives and hope and pray for the best, not when it comes to racism.

No tech stack, no matter what they promise you, is going to magically de-bias your entire recruitment process, nor give you defined problem statements to allow you to ensure you are putting in interventions that make a difference and dismantle systemic racism. That's the key piece that is often missed.

There are those who advocate that diversity and inclusion has done more harm than good for Black people, and I understand exactly what they mean.

Let me explain.

The Origins of Diversity and Inclusion

Diversity education was originally a reaction to the civil rights movement in the 1960s as a way to increase awareness of the inequalities Black people face in all facets of society, from work and education to housing, justice and medical care. By the 1990s companies, as well as academic institutions, government departments and cultural/heritage organizations, had implemented their own D&I training. But by that point the original diversity education that had been created back in the 1960s to improve Black people's lives within the US (and the UK) had undergone a number of changes.

As education for gender diversity increased in the 1970s and 1980s and barriers to inclusion for other minoritised communities came to the fore in the 1990s, diversity training became part of a catch-all solution for corporates to mitigate legal risk. Consider that between the late 1990s and early 2000s, Bank of America Merrill Lynch paid out almost half a billion US dollars in discrimination claims, Morgan Stanley paid approximately $54 million during the same time period, and Smith Barney paid over $100 million in similar cases (Dobbin and Kalev, 2016). Such eye-wateringly large lawsuits were in part responsible for compelling investment banks and corporates alike to expand D&I training, tighten workplace discrimination policies and add class action, or group litigation, clauses to employment contracts. This forged D&I training into a corporate weapon that commands and controls its colleagues by forbidding workplace bias even though it is systemic: already baked into an organization's operating systems.

In the 1960s diversity training focused solely on racial bias and discrimination against Black people. D&I training today has the lofty aim to be all-embracing, comprehensive in its sweep of removing bias and discriminatory practice against all minoritised communities.

> *I don't want to just focus on race. It makes me feel uncomfortable. What about everyone else?*
> Diversity and inclusion manager, 2021

Understanding the barriers that different minoritised communities face is essential in creating societal equity. Racism, white supremacy and patriarchy are problems in other communities as well, and having insight and acting on the overlapping and interdependent systems of discrimination and disadvantage through intersectionality is vital to ending oppression across social categorisations of humans. Yet the attempt to merge the specific discriminatory issues facing each minoritised community into, for example, one day's annual training, minimises the core inequities each community faces. As it mitigates them, it sanitises personal experiences for accessible, mass consumption by mainly white cisgendered heterosexual able-bodied male colleagues.

The discrimination and bias against minoritised communities is watered down to such an extent that D&I training can carry no transformative meaning for any minoritised community it aims to support. And when an entity takes that approach across its entire D&I agenda, that exacerbates problems rather than alleviating them.

To put it bluntly, racism feeds off our inability to be specific about the structural barriers affecting different ethnic groups. White power structures bank on discomfort about race being so acute that we are conditioned to avoid challenging it and will fight hard to maintain it.

Our society and our workplace cultures reward those who toe the line. To challenge authority and call out wrongdoing is to put a target on your back. It is to be labelled the difficult one, the aggressive one. It is the start of a shortened tenure, exclusions from key meetings, and finding yourself consistently overlooked because you're not seen as a team player.

That is how Black people are oppressed within the workplace. Management may pay lip service to expressed concerns, but that is a fictitious performance. Remind me again about your zero-tolerance approach to racism?

In the sixty years since diversity education was established to advance racial equity for Black people, it has regressed to barely skim over the specific racial discrimination Black colleagues face every day at work. The issues entrenched in workplace systemic racism have been smoothed over and made more agreeable in order to fit the generalised traditional model of D&I education. Rather than promoting equity through pay equality and opportunity, such a model enables companies to issue vague platitudes in their HR policies and corporate messaging about the organization's promotion of diversity and inclusion. In actual fact, however, all they have done is assimilate all minoritised communities into a single homogenised unit of not being 'normal', of being 'othered'.

It also soothes the conscience of decision makers who want to be applauded for doing the right thing, even if the 'right thing' makes no material difference to the people most impacted.

I've told the board this is a marathon, not a sprint, and it will take us a long time to make change. We're expanding into new territories so unfortunately we don't have the resources or money to invest in this issue on its own anymore, so we want to bring it back under our diversity, equity and inclusion strategy. We've learnt a lot in the last eighteen months and I'm thankful for the experience.

CEO, 2021

But you cannot command and control racial bias through rules and an annual day of reeducation or a week of inclusion awareness. This format cannot change the way people think – consciously or subconsciously – and therefore it cannot change organizational systems.

This is why, even with your annual D&I training, your London office is full of white faces. Why there is only one Black person on your board of directors (if you're lucky). And up until now, that's been perfectly fine. All that talk about being representative of the communities you serve is just that: talk.

When you're under pressure to act, the D&I training session isn't the time to think, 'Oh shit, we need more D&I people. More hours of this D&I training. We just need to do more stuff'. All that is basically a form of carrying on doing the same thing, but more of it, merely throwing money at the issues in a spray-and-pray fashion and hoping something sticks. When you as a leader don't really understand it or feel comfortable addressing it, this simplistic approach makes the problem something to be solved by your Black colleagues, your HR department or your D&I lead.

We need to remove the emotion out of it. I think that's part of our challenge here. Our Black colleagues are just too emotional and I feel like we can't do right for doing wrong.

Global chief people officer, 2020

And we got here through rational thinking.

Continuity is key. Embedding such continuity within larger, ongoing structural change makes it part of the company's way of doing business. Traditional D&I commitments are simply a way for an organization to say they don't really want to change; they just want to look like they do, knowingly or not. In doing so your company is tinkering around the edges of advancing racial equity: ticking boxes to show a veneer of responsibility and progressive action, and – fingers crossed – shielding themselves from litigation.

That's what lip service is, isn't it? Doing the bare minimum because you have to, in the hope it all goes away.

> *Okay, so all we have to do is find more Black people and then everyone's happy.*
>
> Chairman, 2020

But this is a wake-up call to awareness that traditional D&I approaches aren't magically going to make things better for Black colleagues, and that your company's traditional D&I training practices and stale HR discrimination policies will not shield you from damaging and costly racial discrimination claims.

> *Does your firm negotiate with racists?*
>
> Shereen Daniels, 2021

Racism and Discrimination Are Illegal in the Eyes of the Law

The main objectives of equality, civil rights and anti-discrimination public policy is to secure free competition between individuals, and eliminate barriers created by discrimination.

In the UK the Equalities Act 2010 prohibits discrimination in the workplace and in wider society. The Act encompasses the following types of discrimination, otherwise known as protected characteristics:

- Age
- Gender reassignment
- Being married or in a civil partnership
- Being pregnant or on maternity leave
- Disability
- Race, including colour, nationality, ethnic or national origin
- Religion or belief
- Sex
- Sexual orientation

If you have any of these protected characteristics, the Equalities Act 2010 is meant to protect you:

- At work
- In education
- As a consumer
- When using public services
- When buying or renting property
- As a member or guest of a private club or association

The Act recognises that individuals can be discriminated in one or more of the following forms:

- Direct discrimination: treating someone with a protected characteristic less favourably than others

- Indirect discrimination: putting rules or arrangements in place that apply to everyone, but that put someone with a protected characteristic at an unfair disadvantage
- Harassment: unwanted behaviour linked to a protected characteristic that violates someone's dignity or creates an offensive environment for them
- Victimisation: treating someone unfairly because they've complained about discrimination or harassment.

However, the enacting of such legislation within company policy does not eradicate racial discrimination in the workplace.

You don't need to consult your HR person for the detail to know that discrimination happens within your business. Racism happens within your business. It makes no difference whether or not it was intentional.

Even though the legislation is there, it is wilful ignorance to assume that its mere presence and your subsequent HR policies and procedures offer adequate protection for your Black colleagues.

We've audited our policies and procedures and have a consultant updating them now. I'm confident this will make a difference. It's a start at least.

People and culture director, 2021

In 2019 a University of Manchester study involving more than 5,000 people into workplace racism concluded that over 70% of participating workers from 'ethnic communities' had experienced racial harassment at work within the past five years, with 60% subjected to racism by their employer. Almost half reported racism had negatively impacted their ability to do their job (University of Manchester, 2021).

Employment tribunals in the UK reported a 48% increase in the number of race discrimination claims in 2020. Some notable claims made the press:

The Department for Work and Pensions was ordered to pay a former trainee £400,000 after a judge ruled her colleagues created a 'hostile environment' of racism and ageism that forced her out of her job (Gayle, 2021).

Two former British Army soldiers won a racial discrimination claim against the Ministry of Defence (MoD) after the judge ruled that they had been victims of racist graffiti written on a photo of them. The tribunal also pointed out that there was a significantly disproportionate number of complaints of racial or sexual discrimination stemming from the MoD (Mangion, 2021).

In no uncertain terms, your company needs to meet its legal duties and ensure that organizational policies are in line with key legal expectations. However, as the University of Manchester study demonstrates, legally mandated anti-discrimination workplace policies don't reduce racial discrimination, unfair treatment and inequity. As previously highlighted, this is a result of the fact that discrimination is a societal problem, as well as a political one, meaning the top-down approach implicit in legislation that feeds into workplace policy and procedure has limitations. It can't shift individual behaviours, attitudes and hundreds of years of societal racial bias that is baked into corporate systems and process. In addition, it operates within a power structure that was deliberately set up to preserve, uphold and protect the majority.

Think about how your anti-discrimination policies are applied and upheld within your organization. Do you hold everyone to the same standards? For whom do you make exceptions? Whom do you protect? Why do your policies apply to some people and others not all?

Dismantling systemic racism goes far beyond simply avoiding legal liability.

How Robust Is Your First Line of Defence?

In the University of Manchester study, over 40% of those who reported a racist incident said they were either ignored or subsequently identified as a 'trouble maker', with more than one in ten of those who raised a complaint of racial harassment subsequently disciplined or forced out of their job (University of Manchester, 2021).

When a Black employee raises a racist incident through their organization's appropriate channel, the degree to which they are supported in the process is based on whether their manager or HR leader, who is likely to be white, believes that there is a racist element, understanding that a white employee, regardless of title or department, will not have lived experience of racial abuse. Their reality, societal and workplace positioning means they have no point of reference to understand racial abuse. Yet the validity of a workplace racist incident is based on whether they do, on whether a Black employee can convince a white manager that what they are saying is true.

In fact, rather than seek to listen, or to self-examine how custom and practice had perpetuated racism and discrimination, HR leaders themselves joined the bandwagon in gaslighting their colleagues.

We have over the last few weeks received an increasing number of BAME [Black, Asian and Minority Ethnic; the use of this acronym further illustrates this manager's lack of awareness] staff saying that they are being discriminated against. We have looked carefully into each one of these, and we can find no evidence of them being discriminated against. It 'feels like' (no evidence to prove this), when a BAME member of staff gets an answer that they do not like, they instantly claim discrimination. I am trying to put a grievance response together and then a manager wants to say something along the lines of 'your spurious claims of racial discrimination are causing disruption to the business and taking up valuable time which could be better utilised' but I feel this may add fuel to the fire.

HR manager via an open HR forum, 2021

Moving Black colleagues into a space where the validation or invalidation of their lived experience depends on convincing white people that the issue is real. When racism is not your lived experience and you're not properly trained to pay attention to what that lived experience looks like, you are likely to pass off, for example, racist verbal abuse as nothing more than 'banter', encouraging colleagues to 'lighten up'. In the aforementioned University of Manchester report, *nearly 50% of respondents were subjected to 'verbal abuse and racist jokes'* (University of Manchester, 2021.

You'll waste time looking for concrete evidence and, coupled with your discomfort in talking about race and wanting to believe in the inherent 'goodness' of your colleagues, you'll side with the alleged perpetrators because you see this issue only through your own experience and limited knowledge.

When a Black employee's experience doesn't qualify for being taken seriously, that reduces their value as an employee and as a person. They can't be their authentic self at work when their experience within the workplace is disregarded. They are not respected, which in turn means that they are not comfortable sharing their creative ideas; thus systemic racism prevents them from adding value to the overall objective of the organization.

We don't matter. Not as much as white colleagues who are far more valuable as proven by the disproportionate amount of energy and effort companies place on ensuring they don't feel left out of commitments to diversity and inclusion.

Ultimately racism leaves money on the table, in many different guises. Yet more than that, it's profoundly unfair.

Allay (UK) Limited v Mr S Gehlen

As a UK employer, you can be held liable for the acts of colleagues, regardless of whether you endorsed or were even aware of the behaviour in the first place. The only way to protect yourself is by demonstrating that you took all reasonable steps to prevent the harassment from occurring. In February 2021, an Employment Appeals Tribunal (EAT) found that Allay (UK) Ltd could not rely upon an 'all reasonable steps' defence to a claim of racial harassment when the training the company provided to its colleagues, less than two years prior, was deemed 'stale' by the EAT.

In the facts about the case, Mr Gehlen (self-described as a gentleman of Indian origin) was employed as a senior analyst at Allay (UK) Ltd between 3 October 2016 and 15 September 2017, when his employment was terminated on grounds of poor performance. Following his dismissal, Mr Gehlen submitted a complaint to his former employer, stating that he had been subject to harassment on the grounds of his race by one of his peers, Mr Pearson. Allay (UK) Ltd carried out an investigation into the complaint and found that Mr Pearson had indeed made racist comments on a regular basis about Mr Gehlen to the effect that Mr Gehlen should work in a corner shop, that he drove a Mercedes 'like all Indians' and that he had been asked why he was in the country. As a result, Mr Pearson was ordered to undertake further training on equality and diversity by the company, which Allay (UK) Ltd deemed effective. The EAT did not:

> *However, it appears in this case that Mr Pearson, despite having undergone the training, thought that what he was doing was no more than "banter". That provided some further evidence that the training that was provided had faded from his memory. The Tribunal was also entitled to conclude the fact that managers did not know what to do when they observed harassment, or it was reported to them, suggested that the training had also faded from their memories.*
>
> *Allay (UK) Ltd v Mr S Gehlen, 2021, p. 14*

Underlying that finding is the obvious point that the less effective the training is, the more quickly it becomes stale, making traditional tick-box diversity training insufficient to establish a defence to workplace racial harassment. Allay (UK) Limited v Mr S Gehlen is the wake-up call for employers to move beyond the traditional corporate mindset that sees discrimination as a compliance problem, to a new mindset where inclusiveness pervades all the aspects of the workplace. This requires thinking outside the legal framework and recognising the limitations of how little protection is actually afforded to Black and minoritised colleagues.

What Next?

If your company's governance structure remains at threshold, so you don't learn how to hire, reward and promote Black colleagues; train all staff to recognise the interplay of racism, privilege and power; or even communicate intent, then you are actively making the decision to increase corporate risk profile. Such a decision also reduces profit, investor interest and employee input, as well as increases exposure to legal action. This is a ruinous business plan.

It is time to future-proof. And by that I don't mean study and talk the issues of advancing racism to death. Don't get bogged down in the definitions. Yes, research it, talk about it and discuss concerns, but at some point you have to be able to draw a line and say, 'This is what we are going to do and this is how we're going to get there', and marry the two together in order to move towards tangible action.

Your time for merely talking is done.

So organizations talk about innovation and ideas – pipelines of business development projects and experimentation. When you experiment you're testing a hypothesis, often very quickly without having all the facts because you're looking to see, 'If we do X what happens, what's the impact?' And if your experiment works and produces a better customer experience, that leads to more profit.

This experimentation and creative thinking is the same process that allows companies to pivot quickly, to quickly react to change. So why do you throw all of that creativity and experimentation out the window when it comes to dismantling systemic racism in your workplace?

Why do you want to sit, and think, and mull it over, and discuss, and reflect. . .and we're still waiting. You don't need to be sitting for a month, or next quarter, or next year to decide what you're going to do about systemic racism.

You need to hold up a mirror and say, 'What's stopping us from properly addressing this now?'

Shereen Daniels

Your Anti-Racist Leadership Starts Now

Progressive leaders for today and the future commit to seeing how the social construct of race is used to isolate, disadvantage and make power inaccessible to Black people. They are alert to unequal outcomes and work to dismantle systematic racism within their organization and areas of influence.

This commitment is not performative diversity without accountability (e.g. the occasional company policy or social media post). It is an ongoing leadership practice that judges every company decision against its potential racist or anti-racist impact, one that is visible to colleagues, stakeholders and clients, actively guiding the organization towards greater equity.

The new model of leadership doesn't need the title of anti-racism or racial equity. Instead, it is baked in – a core capability, if you like. It becomes the standard.

When my advisory firm, HR rewired, begin helping to shape organizations' leadership approach to this, we discovered they often see anti-racism as something separate, an addition to – rather than an essential part of – how they do business.

There are three main traits that I believe distinguish the leaders who have what it takes to implement intentional and consistent steps to dismantle systemic racism – not because they have all the knowledge and expertise, but because they know how to get things done through people. They ask the right questions, centre others rather than themselves, and are adept at navigating complex and ambiguous situations. In addition to this, they show humility, moral courage and tenacity:

- *Humility* is the quality or state of not thinking you are better than other people; thus you are able to create space for people to feel like they are of equal value. You do not lead with your job title or status.
- *Moral courage* means taking action because it's the right thing to do and remaining firm in the face of discomfort and opposition. It's easy to be a leader when you're popular, when others around you feel exactly the same as you do. It's harder when you're facing into issues that address aspects of who we are that most people prefer to leave unexplored.
- *Tenacity* is the ability to persist with a course of action even if there is no immediate payoff or reward. Recognise that change doesn't happen overnight, and neither can it neatly fit your strategy planning cycles.

Take a moment and think about you and individuals around your leadership table. How far do you embody these traits? How far do they? Do you think it matters?

With these leadership traits as the bedrock of dismantling systemic racism, it becomes part and parcel of the way you do business to regularly ask questions like these:

- How far does this decision alleviate or worsen inequality?
- If we don't do X, what is the impact on Y?
- Who are the consistent winners and losers here?
- What other patterns or trends should we watch out for?
- How far are we doing what's comfortable versus what's right?

Yet in commencing a path of anti-racism, leaders get caught up with concerns based on the 'appropriateness' of when and how they should commit to anti-racism. They often treat it as a separate programme or initiative that is divorced from business as usual, that eventually has an expiry date. It's difficult to sustain the energy and momentum to address issues that directly don't affect you, isn't it?

Therefore, the question considering an appropriate time to commence action predetermined by a suitable attainment of appropriate information/training/guidance/divine intervention is one bound by privilege, by centring safety and comfort for the majority.

Consider it this way. Your Black colleagues were ready yesterday. They were ready last week, last month, last year and the year before that. Not sure if you have an issue with racism in your business? Contemplate the obvious and look around you.

Looking at Your Surroundings

If you consider the demographic composition of your town or city, is its ethnic reality reflected within your company? From this you may determine that assumptions are made in your organization about who is an employee, who gets to be an employee, and why this is the way it is. Think truthfully about what you assume to be the reasons and barriers for Black people to be excluded either from employment, retention or progression within your organization.

Because, let's face it, most corporate colleagues are white, most corporate executives are white, and this demographic didn't wind up so white without a lot of unfairness and discrimination, unless you are of the opinion that it just so happens that all the talented and capable leaders are white – and male.

So, at the outset of questioning your company's partnership with systemic racism and your leadership within the affiliation, start with the obvious. Look around you and ask why.

Recognising Fear-Based Beliefs

It has never been more important for companies to engage authentically in difficult conversations about racial equity and systemic change, yet corporate leaders hesitate. More often than not this is related to fear, and to be honest, fear is really the operative emotion we're working with right now. It's a reason why many companies have not gone down this path before.

But to truly create change, those in leadership need to work through their discomfort and reexamine their views and actions. Silence doesn't challenge systemic racism. And fear can direct views and actions that, even unintentionally, can have a profound impact on whether Black colleagues feel connected and empowered, or pushed aside, held back and excluded.

Corporate leaders are generally 'fix-it' people, with a desire for strategy (i.e. 'Just tell me what to do'). Yet recognising fear-based beliefs around systemic racism is emotional work for white leaders. It's uncomfortable and always contains a desire to move onto something more concrete, something more comfortable. In such moments it's worth considering that white people don't have to think or talk about race. You can go through life without dealing with it. It's a choice you have. It's not a choice Black people have. Therefore, as corporate leaders you need to interrupt your pattern of thinking and consider new patterns, ones that address the systems of power that oppress certain people and advantage others within their workplace.

Within this concept are three main fear-related barriers to anti-racist leadership.

There isn't a problem   This fear-related barrier is based on meritocratic ideology, on the illusion of opportunity equality. This idea assumes that every employee has the same chance to succeed within a firm as long as they work hard enough, and that there is no bias built into the system and if there is, it has a negligible impact on colleagues. Yet success does not equate to having a superior or inferior work ethic, and such meritocratic criteria within a workplace diverts attention from the systemic structures and conditions that are making it impossible for Black people to succeed. A corporate structural demographic is not simply a reflection of variation in individual talent and effort, because it negates long-standing disparities within the distribution of resources and life chances for Black people.

If you have surveyed your organization and discovered that its demographic doesn't reflect the ethnic reality outside its front door, then you have a systemic racism problem. This shortcoming is an effective indicator that meritocracy is not an equity solution.

A common counter-question from many business leaders is the assumption that the push for diversifying teams is more important than 'merit', and to them this feels like a backwards step. Not only does this question assume that the two objectives are mutually exclusive, but it betrays just how wedded they are to the idea that white leaders are inherently more superior, qualified and capable.

At a senior level, most of the hiring decisions are made within a pool of friendship and peer networks, often referred to as the 'hidden job market'. Therefore, it is a function of your network, your social capital, rather than meritocracy, that is a critical element of hiring and promotional decision-making.

> *The UK government's white paper on auditing and corporate governance ("Restoring confidence in UK corporate controls", FT View, March 19) presents boards with an interesting dilemma. Nominations committees will need to apply their very best wisdom to reconciling two opposing requirements: to continue improving the diversity of the board on the one hand, and to appoint directors who are qualified to take much greater responsibility for the accuracy of company accounts on the other.*
>
> *While non-executive directors must of course fulfil their duties relating to corporate reporting and audit, making it easier to prosecute them is unlikely to help attract more diverse candidates into the role. Quite the opposite.*
>
> *An effective board comprises a mixture of financial experts, professionals with sector knowledge and directors from other backgrounds who bring diverse perspectives. It was never easy for chairs to get that mix right.*
>
> *If these proposals are confirmed, it will become harder still.*
>
> Letter to the Financial Times (Bamford
> and Dawkins, 2021)

There's no benefit in talking   White people are generally uncomfortable talking about race, unconscious biases and privileges (though not as uncomfortable as it is to live through and experience racism), but there is great benefit in talking.

Numerous historical moments illustrate where progress has only been made because conversations were had, such as (amongst many other examples) universal suffrage, gender equality and marriage equality. None of these things were achieved through comfort and silence. Conversations were started, were continued and are still being had to ensure they continue to progress. Those with moral courage, irrespective of their job title and rank within the workplace and society, pushed through any discomfort to advocate for change. The more conversations, the more likely change will happen.

There will be negative consequences   The fear of negative consequences suggests the potential of damaging relationships for saying the wrong thing, for making mistakes, alienating white colleagues or even triggering PR disaster.

Compare the risk of anti-racist leadership to that of company innovation. When it comes to innovation, the possibility of failure is outweighed by the need to future-proof. When it comes to an organizational sea change to lead fairly, the argument is the same: the potentiality of failure is outweighed by the need to future-proof the organization. The business case for anti-racist leadership is one previously presented and one to be reckoned with.

In acknowledging and confronting your own fear, an anti-racist leader recognises how ill-equipped most white colleagues are to confront systemic racism. Yet permission can't be given to white people to escape or avoid challenges to their privilege; this would be a privilege unto itself. To begin to address corporate systemic racism requires that you visibly do the work yourself. Experience your discomfort in an honest and forthright way, accept that you won't be perfect, but commit to doing better.

Changing Fear-Based Beliefs

Leadership is about inspiring others to make a vision become reality, and a company can never improve unless its leaders first improve themselves. Therefore, in order to make it safe for others to speak and enable idea generation to shape and form, change must start from the top – change that is coupled with intention, commitment and then action. Dismantling systemic racism in the workplace starts with you.

Be willing to disrupt dominant power structures that inhibit change. Whilst it isn't all on you, sometimes it's necessary to go out and on a limb and be the first. Denying your power is untrue, and coming up with a list of things that you can't do and why is still rooted in fear.

If you are a white leader, whether you like it or not, you reflect and reinforce the dominant culture. It shapes how you view normal, good, bad, effective, comfortable, convenient or risky. Confronting fear-based beliefs is just the painful beginning, yet it's a practice that requires ongoing attention to reinforce personal values and commitment to corporate leadership.

To move beyond recognition to changing fear-based beliefs requires leaders to sit comfortably with discomfort. Acknowledging that you don't have to have all the answers, fear of saying or doing the wrong thing, a question of what is appropriate and the fear of taking things 'too far' shouldn't stop you from trying to dismantle racism within your company, should it?

You don't have to have all the answers to care.
                    Jon Wilson, CEO, Stepstone Atlantic

References

Allay (UK) Ltd v Mr S Gehlen, UKEAT/0031/20/AT Judgement (Employment Appeal Tribunal 2021).

Bamford, Tessa, and Dawkins, Will. (24 March 2021). Letter: Audit reform may stall boards' diversity drive. Retrieved from https://www.ft.com/content/4f8e0dfb-3eac-49e3-a3d3-72cbcf180f50.

Discrimination: your rights. (2021). Retrieved 14 September 2021, from https://www.gov.uk/discrimination-your-rights/how-you-can-be-discriminated-against.

Dobbin, Frank, and Kalev, Alexandra. (July–August 2016). Why Diversity Programs Fail. Retrieved 15 September 2021, from https://hbr.org/2016/07/why-diversity-programs-fail.

Equality Act 2010. (2010). https://www.legislation.gov.uk/ukpga/2010/15/contents.

Gayle, Damien. (25 February 2021). DWP ordered to pay former trainee £400k over racism and ageism. Retrieved 14 September 2021, from https://www.theguardian.com/uk-news/2020/feb/25/dwp-ordered-to-pay-former-trainee-400k-over-racism-and-ageism.

Hobbes, Thomas. (1651). *Leviathan or The Matter, Forme and Power of a Commonwealth Ecclesiasticall and Civil.*

Locke, John. (1690). *An Essay Concerning Human Understanding.*

Mangion, David. (2021). 12 Notorious UK Discrimination Cases. Retrieved 14 September 2021, from https://www.skillcast.com/blog/12-notorious-uk-discrimination-cases.

Newkirk, Pamela. (2019). Diversity Has Become a Booming Business. So Where Are the Results? Retrieved 15 September 2021, from https://time.com/5696943/diversity-business/.

University of Manchester (15 April 2021). Racism is still a huge problem in UK's workplaces, finds report. Retrieved 14 September 2021, from https://www.manchester.ac.uk/discover/news/racism-is-still-a-huge-problem/.

White people who grew up in low-income families or didn't experience 'the good life', what does white privilege mean to you and how do you feel about the term?
Question posted on AskReddit

I honestly think it is even more noticeable. I was orphaned at 12. Had no stability and was always on the edge of being sent to the household of a different relative. I was a good kid. When you are given no rules but know if [you] bring any trouble to attention you are moving – you are amazingly good. I did well in school and had a scholarship.

But the lack of a familial support system throughout made everything a tightrope. Adults who knew my situation were sympathetic and helpful and I was always surrounded with the expectation that a smart kid like me would make something of myself. I can not express how fragile the tightrope was and the underlying fear I had of the consequences of breaking that image. And with all that I had massive struggles and a few significant failures.

Now take that and begin the tightrope with the adults in schools and teen jobs having other assumptions. If they didn't assume I would, despite no parents nor money, find a way to college. If that wasn't instilled in me. Let me say that I never once thought not going to college was even a possibility. Smart kids went to college. That is how it worked. **Do you really think I would have had that same unshakable perspective if I were not white?** *I certainly don't. And there were very, very few things in my youth that were that certain. Without that certainty, I can't even imagine w[h]ere I would be.*

The people that struggle with white privilege generally have a lot of other privileges too. I expect they think, "well that difference is because the black kid is poor/bad neighbourhood/fatherless not just because their skin is dark." **I can tell you when white privilege is just about the only privilege you have, you don't mistake** *the value of it.* *You ride those positive assumptions about white kids for all they are worth and double down to prove them right.*

The other thing you really notice is that you can "pass" in a way non-white people from a similar background cannot. If I don't want to go into all the hard-luck of my life – then or now – everyone just assumes I have a normal middle-class background. Small slips are overlooked (not knowing what is appropriate to order at a business dinner) because people don't easily challenge their assumptions. I don't need a seminar to know that's not the same for non-white people. Basically I have the privilege of not having to explain how I overcame challenges to get where I am. **My privilege is that people assume I did not have the challenges.** *And I don't know if you can understand how beneficial it is to pass like this. Having to explain it is exhausting no matter what your race. And I am sure the "subtle" probes are very frustrating for non-whites who just had a middle-class upbringing.*

To all the people that say, "There are poor white individuals who have massive struggles how can that be a privilege over X." Yes there are massive struggles that can be experienced by any human. But going through them with dark skin is not the same experience as going through them with white skin. I am in my 40s, so all this "white privilege" talk wasn't anything I heard in my 20s. But I remember a time shortly after college when things just fell apart for me. I was just starting to put things back together – and I don't know why this crossed my mind – but I remember thinking "Thank God at least I am white or this would be even harder." I really don't know what prompted that thought but I remember how obvious that was to me then.

White privilege is among other things the benefit of the doubt. And there were times that this was difference between staying on the tightrope or falling off. The expectation that I would make it to the other side – not just from the teachers and relatives, but every story I read of orphans making good (who all happened to be white). That all pushed me past moments when a more "realistic" expectation would have led me off the tightrope and onto a more "realistic" balance beam with a more "realistic" destination. White privilege is not just external – although it is definitely external – it is also part of our self-image and limits or lack thereof we place on our imagined future. Smart kids go to college. That was my expectation, that rule and my unquestioning perception of that being a rule and not an aspiration shaped my life as strongly as my mother's death did.

And I do not think I am wrong to imagine that non-white kids are not surrounded by such a universal expectation. Even one teacher not behaving as if college were a forgone conclusion for me would have made me start questioning and investigating how unrealistic college would be with no money. And what other options there were. These are things I never considered – not even when I was floundering in college.

Response posted by Oddlikeeveryoneelse (2021)

Defining Meaning

I am a 58-year-old successful white businessman with a great family and network. Everything in my life is safe, secure and comfortable. But George Floyd's murder...

It caused me as a white middle-aged man to ask myself questions I thought I knew the answers to. But my perspective of the world wasn't in sync with reality. I had no idea what the concept of white privilege meant. I had classic liberal privileged views of what the world was like. And asking questions made me uncomfortable.

Understanding what my role was in doing something about it I found difficult to answer. I didn't know how to shape the answers as I didn't have the tools.

But I knew I had to answer the ultimate question, 'Am I going to be on the right side of this, or the wrong side?' Am I going to be a spectator for the change, or help figure out the right things to do?

Chief executive officer, 2021

Using Language as a Tool to Dismantle Racism

A conversation I still have, frequently, concerns language: the words to use and the words not to use. What language is best so as not to alienate the rest of the workforce who we need on our side?

What words can we use instead of 'racism' and 'white supremacy' because it makes people nervous, some find it divisive, and it means we have to stop before we barely get started?

There has been no acknowledgement, no awareness of how the words we use naturalise systemic racism. How our language reinforces power dynamics that are never tipped in favour of Black people.

> *Our CEO doesn't like the word 'anti-racism' or anything that specifically mentions racism. We settled on adding the word 'equity', so now we use diversity, equity and inclusion in our communications.*
>
> Corporate affairs director, 2020

Power is wielded through the use of words to label people, to whitewash racism into phrases and sentences that are softer, seen as more professional or objective.

Such usage distorts meaning and skews reality, all in favour of preserving the status quo. The ultimate result is intended to make life easier and more comfortable for those who wield power, and to continue to oppress those who are most impacted by racism.

Yes, language matters.

I don't even know what we can and can't say anymore. It doesn't make it any easier when you know you can be cancelled by the mob just for saying the wrong thing.

Chief executive officer, 2021

We are all constructed in a world of our creation using one particular kind of language, one we've inherited from institutions, from education systems and workplace conventions that were built on a framework of systemic racism.

Our words perpetuate racist ideology.

If you are so used to saying the same words over and over again, the frequency of their use makes them truisms. And when that occurs we never explore meaning or context, and why certain phrases are used over others in describing Black people or anyone who is deemed different according to the standards of society.

This chapter sets out what is meant by the terminology within this book. Use it as a reference to gain a framework for understanding. It will assist you to consider the appropriateness of the words drafted in your corporate communications, spoken in meetings, used both formally and informally within your workplace. So that every time you use the word Black, emphasise cultural fit, promote integration, consider the phrase white privilege or even question why 'ethnic minority' is written in quotation marks, you understand what it specifically means in a workplace context and the lived experience of your Black colleagues.

The context here isn't about creating an all-inclusive anti-racist dictionary, but one that enables you to dismantle racism and to advance racial equity in the workplace through language, through deliberate, intentional choices about the words you use and their impact.

There are the key terminologies to understand and get comfortable with. Understanding what they mean will help your company's way of thinking and operating to evolve to the extent, it becomes very easy to identify which companies have delved into the roots of racism, reflected, learnt and switched up their language, versus those who have skimmed the surface and held tight to antiquated or exclusionary phrases because it's convenient and fits within comfort levels and risk profiles.

Context is everything. Be willing to challenge what others take for granted. Claiming ignorance is no longer acceptable.

Corporate Regimes of Truth

Words may be speech or writing, images or audiovisual media, symbols or routines: anything that conveys meaning and can be 'read' to be understood or interpreted.

Your organization will have its own words and common language. Some of this is inherited from previous colleagues and leaders, and some created by you and the people you've brought in during your tenure:

Articulate
Professional
Neutral
Natural
Objective
Accepted, therefore, correct

This is your corporate 'regime of truth', the beliefs and knowledge of what is true and what is best practice.

A corporate 'regime of truth' tells colleagues which words and therefore which 'truths' are told, when they are told and by whom, and enables those controlling the words (i.e. white people, the most powerful people in the room) to take for granted the power relations the words are imbued with.

In truth, white people miss the effect of their words and they miss the fact that these effects serve their own interests. So it comes as no surprise that white voices are heard more often, are more likely to be believed and are given greater status. And when you control all the words and their meaning, you take for granted your power and privilege in social structures, social systems and social expectations.

Majority/Minority

When we talk specifically about the power and privilege encased in language, the phrase 'ethnic minority' and its counterpart, global majority, immediately come to mind.

The words majority/minority are binary opposites so we know what one means because it is the opposite of the other. You can't understand minority without knowing majority. The English language is set up for binary dichotomies – two distinct opposing words understood through difference in degrees (rather than difference in kind). And the pairs are always ranked, with one part having higher value and privilege over the other (e.g. man/woman, white/ Black, heterosexual/homosexual, majority/minority). The first word in the binary is generally given more status or advantage, and understood as original, normal and superior.

But this is a social construct. It's not true.

What is true is that the minoritised communities that make up the 'ethnic minority' are not in the minority. Statistically they are the global majority.

I never thought about the use of the word 'minority' before. What you're saying makes sense. But I don't like the term global majority. It feels like a threat to me.
LinkedIn comment, 2021

If the knowledge that white people are the global minority makes you feel uncomfortable, it is possibly because it highlights that the social conventions signposting your understanding of the world, the ones that benefit you above all else, are false. And the words you use to describe yourself, and your position in the world, no longer hold up. Your understanding of normal has been changed, and perhaps for the first time you see systemic racism encased within words.

This example demonstrates binary hierarchy within language to be socially produced, and therefore not inevitable or accidental and, unlike knowing 'London is the capital of England', not factual.

Diverse

Another word to consider is diverse. Diverse is an 'othering' word, an identity of difference constructed to produce cultural standards of normality and superiority (i.e. we are normal; they are diverse). It produces an identity difference between people to exclude or 'other' those who are not 'like us'. In systemic racism, it favours white people, because the word is typically used to describe anyone who isn't white. So by definition, white becomes normal, the standard.

I was born in the UK, a Black British woman of Afro-Caribbean heritage. Yet in the workplace, I will be defined and described as the diverse hire. Not because of my gender, nor my place of birth, but because of my skin colour.

When you're describing another person, it is a given that they are white if you highlight their hair colour, height, dress sense, job title or department they work in. A Black employee will be described by their skin colour first.

You don't know Marcus in HR? The tall Black guy?

What's her name in marketing? You know the Black woman who's always smiling?

When you use words to 'other', you are constructing a reality based on hierarchical privilege, rather than representing actual reality. You are using socially produced concepts, generally based on political (the norms and standards) gain, to exclude people who don't look like you.

We are all diverse.

'Majority/minority' and 'diverse' are just two examples of common words and phrases used across educational systems, the media and the workplace that aren't questioned because they don't negatively impact white people. However, they give insight to the social construction of language, the power and privilege behind words and some understanding about why words really do matter.

Talk about diversifying your teams (the action) rather than use the term diverse (as a label).

Define Your Language. Be specific.

Scrutinising your language choices and learning to pull apart the equity meaning, the social conventions, fixed in your language can tactically disrupt racial inequity within your organization.

Deconstructing communication helps you to understand the 'regime of truth' your business is built upon. It shows up the cracks, the contradictions and relationships with power. It questions the meanings of words or concepts (policies, practices, communication) that are normally unquestioned, allowing you to query who benefits and how assumptions about the world are embedded in those systems of thought.

It enables you to consider:

- How did the social conventions within my words, and within my company's communications, come to be?
- Why are we uncomfortable with using certain words and more comfortable with others? What is the unintended consequence of that?
- Why do I take this particular action or use this particular knowledge?
- Whose interests does this knowledge or action serve?
- Who benefits from what I say, do and know?
- How and why do they benefit?

Being curious about terminology will enable you to choose new, kinder and equitable words. And mean them.

A New Terminology

For white people, recognising that the words they use to construct reality are not in fact based on truth but on a social, political and economic agenda that commenced in the seventeenth century can be a lot to take in. It undermines everything previously known to be true, consciously and subconsciously, about reality. It is overwhelming to acknowledge that the fabric of our society and our everyday interactions within the institutions that direct our lives actually perpetuate a 500-year-old lie that we all maintain, ensuring that racism persists as an accepted culture of prejudice, discrimination and exclusivity.

But compared to the results of a YMCA study into the lives of 500 young Black people in 2000, any discomfort felt by this new understanding is insignificant to that of the 95% of young Black people who have witnessed or heard racist language at school (emphasis added):

> *Young Black people shared experiences of other White students telling them in the presence of teachers that "***Black skin is not desirable***", and shared experiences of other students calling them derogatory names. Young Black people felt that racism could be veiled as a joke and shared their experiences of hearing what they described as "subtle racism", whereby* **students and teachers would joke about stereotypes** *associated with young Black people....*
>
> *... Half of young Black people (50%) believe that* **teachers' perceptions of them are one of the biggest barriers to their achievement in school***.*
>
> *In the focus group on education young Black people shared that in British society,* **the definition of a "Black boy" or "Black girl" has already been decided***. Young Black people felt that* **society typically views them as "the class clown" or "underachiever"***. As a result, young Black people explained that* **some teachers automatically view young Black people as "less capable", "unintelligent" and "aggressive"***. Other young Black people in the focus group spoke of instances where they had achieved academic success, and teachers told them that they are* **"surprised at their success"** *or that they are* **"rare"***, emphasising that they should be proud because their success is not common among young Black people.*
>
> YMCA, 2020

And before 47% of young Black people change their name on their CV and 70% have felt the need to change their hair because they are worried about employment bias, concerned that there will be prejudice based on ethnicity when looking for work, institutional, individual and systemic racism has already disempowered them – before they even interview for a job with your organization.

Words matter.

So when you're telling everyone you value authenticity and you want people to bring their full selves into work, do you really mean it? Because to do so is to embrace their lived experiences and also to recognise how the words you use to describe them, the challenges they face because of the their skin colour, can easily disempower, disengage and exclude them, thus affecting your bottom line.

Consider your terminology. Be intentional in how you communicate both internally and externally. Ensure that you understand context, nuance and why certain words should be used above others and what they mean.

Take the time to review your communications through an equity lens. Don't rely on your communications manager, corporate affairs director or PR firm to do this for you, particularly if they don't have both the lived and the professional experience. They are unlikely to clock the nuances we're talking about here.

Doing this properly means you're not risking your reputation, and your brand's reputation purely from a position of ignorance. You're also not causing any more harm.

And that's just as important, if not more so.

The Words

This section is all about moving away from ignorance, to provoke thought and curiosity to understand more. From this point you will be increasingly aware of key terminologies. More importantly, you will be increasingly comfortable using them, and your journey towards racial equity will begin to evolve.

But be warned, from this point on, ignorance will no longer be tolerated as an excuse.

And the last time I looked, Google is still free.

Anti-Black Racism

Racism specifically directed towards Black people, a term mainly used in the US to acknowledge the unique and specific history of African-American people.

See also **Racism**.

Anti-Racism

Acknowledgement of the permanence of racism through organizations, industries and communities, and recognising it as a system of unequal opportunity and punishment based on skin colour.

An anti-racist organization will acknowledge systemic racism within the workplace, from individual workers to C-suite leaders, as well as the ways wealth inequality in society may impact their bottom line though their consumer base. Anti-racist leaders take such evaluations and examine where in the work experience they can actively make existing systems of oppression equitable by opening up paths of opportunity to workers who previously didn't have access to them.

An anti-racist response requires everyday focus from within corporates, and personal responsibility from individuals to act. It requires embedding into our lives so that our perceptions change, and social and workplace interactions become equitable. But such systemic change will only happen when all parts of the system change with it. This is a description of real change rather than tokenism, beyond press releases, donations to charities and the revision of diversity policies.

Disrupting white corporate supremacy will require deep listening, learning and action. It necessitates commitment to being *for* something rather than telling people about what the company is *against*: for white leaders to become comfortable with their discomfort and be accountable for change.

See also **Racism**.

Assimilation

The expectation for Black people to adopt behavioural traits of the majority to fit in and be accepted within the dominant group. This usually means foregoing our cultural identity for fear of exclusion, ridicule or being the centre of unwanted attention.

See also **Integration; Microaggressions**.

BAME

Acronym for Black, Asian, Minority Ethic.

Delete from existence. Only use this term within historical context, and even then put the acronym in inverted commas.

See also **'Ethnic Minority'**.

BIPOC

People of Color. Often used in the US in the same way the UK may use the acronym BAME; however, many people use this phrase and it doesn't have quite the same negative connotations as BAME.

Black

See page 98.

Brown

Brown is a racial term used in the same connotations as Black or white people. Depending on which part of the world you reside, Brown could refer to people from Latin America, for example, whilst in the UK we typically refer people with an Indian heritage background as Brown, or Asian.

Colourblind

See page 103.

Colourism

See page 106.

Diverse

Simply put, a person can't be 'diverse'. This catchall word is a microaggression that positions white people as the default and everyone else as 'other'. It describes Black people as divergent to a standard of human normality (i.e. white guys) – for example, saying that a Black woman is a 'diverse hire'.

Diversity

An ideology that enables white people to superficially commit to advancing racial equity. It considers intentions rather than outcomes, and gives no insight into how individuals will take specific action to promote inclusion. It focuses on representation rather than equity, a tokenistic approach that leaves workplace systems and values unchanged.

It is not possible to have diversity until your organization has authentic inclusion. And it is not possible for your organization to be inclusive unless you have taken specific action to deal with exclusion.

See also **Inclusion**.

Equity and Equality

Equity

Involves giving people what they need to achieve their fullest potential within the workplace.

Acknowledge that the playing field is not level and that opportunities are not equally and fairly distributed.

Equality

In contrast, equality aims to ensure that everyone gets the same things in order to achieve their fullest potential within the workplace. Like equity, equality aims to promote fairness and justice, but it can only work if everyone starts from the same place and needs the same things.

Equality will not advance racial equity. Equality is the destination. Equity is how we get there.

Systemic equity

A complex combination of interrelated elements consciously designed to create, support and sustain racial equity in the workplace. It is a dynamic process that reinforces and replicates equitable ideas, power, resources, strategies, conditions, habits and outcomes.

People with power, rank and privilege generally and genuinely are not anti-equality, but are often anti-equity because they don't like the idea of systems being put into place that will benefit people other than themselves and where they are not included.

The exception to that seems to be gender equality. The push for gender representation doesn't seem to generate the same level of angst, discomfort and backlash, possibly because most gender initiatives are focused exclusively on progressing white women into positions of power without conscious effort to include Black women.

The 2020 annual FTSE report (sponsored by EY) has a picture of two Black people on the front cover of their report, with a Black woman prominently taking centre stage. The report is 52 pages long and the only mention of Black women and barriers to progression to board positions is on page 41, and it's not even a full page (Ernst & Young, 2021).

See also **Human Capital; Power, Rank and Privilege**.

'Ethnic Minority'

Language is moving away from generalising people as an 'ethnic minority'. Like 'BAME', this term is a nod to the past and is to be avoided. If it does appear, it should only do so in inverted commas to highlight the fact that it is outdated. Statistically, the phrase is incorrect.

See also **Global Majority; Individualism; Meritocracy; Minoritised Communities**.

Gaslighting

A situation where the reality and perception of Black employees is questioned, belittled, ignored or overlooked because it does not match the beliefs or views of white people. It is a form of psychological abuse whose purpose is to manipulate and control a person by forcing them to question their thoughts, memories or events that have happened to them.

Gaslighting is also used as a way to silence the voices of Black employees to preserve the ease and comfort of white employees, blaming them for speaking up rather than addressing the wider societal and organizational culture that allows racism and discrimination to flourish unchallenged.

> *'Are you sure you he meant it like that?'*
> *'I know what they did was wrong, but you could have handled it better'.*
> *'It was horrible what happened to George Floyd but let's remember, he was a criminal'.*
> *'I don't recall her saying that. Are you sure you didn't imagine it?'*
> *'Yes but what proof do you have? I can't only take your word for it'.*
> *'We've never had a problem here before. I think you're over exaggerating. It's just a one-off incident.'*
> *'All lives matter.'*

Global Majority

If you require a collective noun to define non-white people – and really, first question whether it's absolutely necessary (for a detailed insight about why, please see page 98) – then consider using global majority. Coined by Rosemary Campbell-Stephens, MBA, to refer to people who are Black,

Asian, Brown, dual-heritage, Indigenous to the global south and/or have been racialised as 'ethnic minorities', 'BAME', 'visible minorities' or 'people of colour', or other terms used to define all non-white people that normalise white and consider everyone else as 'diverse' and not normal.

Global majority, as well as being statistically valid, is a term of empowerment and refuses the deficit narrative of Black people. I am well aware this will make some people feel very uncomfortable.

See also **BAME; 'Ethnic Minority'; Global Majority; Minoritised Communities**.

Human Capital

Once synonymous with slavery, human capital is the off-balance-sheet economic value of an employee's experience, such as education, training and skills. The concept of human capital recognises that not all labour is equal but employers can improve the quality of human capital by investing in colleagues to increase productivity and therefore profitability.

Human capital racial discrimination is a pattern of racial mistreatment that deprives Black colleagues from accessing substantive work opportunities crucial to their professional development and career advancement.

See also **Equity and Equality; Individualism; Meritocracy**.

Inclusion

A work environment that makes every employee feel valued while acknowledging their differences and how these differences contribute to the organization's culture and business outcomes. An inclusive workplace is proactive, where any impact of bias/discrimination/unequal opportunity is negated. An inclusive workplace celebrates diversity and its role within the fabric of the organization. These companies do not pretend that everyone enjoys an equal footing or a level playing field. Instead, they acknowledge differences and systemic racism, taking responsibility to offer equitable opportunities to all.

See also **Diversity**.

Individualism

A condition driven by self-interest: 'This doesn't affect me' or 'How does this affect me?' 'Why should I care?' or 'What's in it for me?'

A Black person who offers their perspective as a racialised individual might be met with discomfort, defensiveness or denial as a way to silence or make invisible how race and racism operate within the organization. Individualism is strongly linked to the meritocracy myth.

See also **Equity and Equality; Human Capital; Meritocracy**.

Integration

An expectation for Black people to mould and adjust themselves and their expectations to fit into the dominant society or culture.

See also **Assimilation**.

Intersectionality

A phrase originally coined in 1989 by civil rights advocate and scholar Kimberlé Crenshaw to describe how race, class, gender and other individual characteristics connect and overlap with one another.

It was, and still is, co-opted as part of broader diversity and inclusion initiatives, with the original premise of the oppression of African-American women frequently and in some cases deliberately left out.

Meritocracy

Meritocracy is the idea that power, privilege and wealth are afforded to those who have earned it on the basis of individual achievement, hard work and/or inherent superiority. Operating within this rationale is the belief that those who are disenfranchised, powerless and/or marginalised (i.e. Black people) are as such due to a personal failure, a refusal to work hard and/or inherent inferiority. The belief in meritocracy handily erases structural inequality, which has a real impact on Black people's power and position today.

See also **Equity and Equality; Human Capital; Individualism**.

Microaggression

Thinly veiled instances of racism.

Microaggressions are more than just insults, insensitive comments or generalised foolish behaviour. They're something very specific: the kinds of remarks, questions or actions that are painful because they have to do with a Black person being a member of a racialised group that's discriminated against or subject to stereotypes. A key part of what makes microaggressions so disconcerting is that they happen casually, frequently and often without any harm intended, in everyday life. They are often passed off as jokes or 'banter' with the victim considered to be 'oversensitive'. Within the workplace the seriousness of a complaint concerning micro-aggression is often left to be decided by a white person in a position of authority.

Minoritised Communities

Groups of communities defined as 'minorities' by white people. The power relationship involves making the 'smaller' group feel that they are somehow 'other' and therefore 'less'. The othering and resulting discrimination are historical, structural and institutional oppression.

See also **BAME; 'Ethnic Minority'; Global Majority**.

Patriarchy

An ideology that men are the natural leaders of the home and society with the ability to wield power and authority indiscriminately.

See also **White Supremacy**.

Performative Allyship

Centring whiteness through self-gratification rather than considering responsibility within a community. It is disingenuous; for example, posting a black square on Instagram is not being an effective ally. It is a performance of personal gratification, centring whiteness. Performative allyship is done to make yourself feel better, to 'prove' you are not a racist, to create a perception of yourself for others, and to be trendy.

An **ally** is a person whose commitment to dismantling oppression is reflected in a willingness to do the following:

- Educate oneself about oppression.
- Learn from and listen to people who are targets of oppression.
- Examine and challenge one's own prejudices, stereotypes and assumptions.
- Work through feelings of guilt, shame and defensiveness to understand what is beneath them and what needs to be healed.
- Learn and practice the skills of challenging oppressive remarks, behaviours, policies and institutional structures.
- Act collaboratively with Black people to dismantle oppression.

See also **Meritocracy; Power, Rank and Privilege**.

Power, Rank and Privilege

Power, rank and privilege operate on personal, interpersonal, cultural and institutional levels and give advantages, favours and benefits to white people at the expense of Black people.

Power

The ability or official authority to decide what is best for others. The ability to decide who will have access to resources. The capacity to exercise control over others and make decisions that impact them without them being in the room.

Rank

The level of seniority a person has within an organization, driven by the job title or grade and where they sit in the official hierarchy, as depicted by your organizational charts – irrespective of how out of date they are!

Privilege

Privilege is characteristically invisible to people who have it. White people often believe that they have earned the privileges that they enjoy or that everyone could have access to these privileges if only they worked to earn them. In fact, privileges are unearned and they are granted to white people whether they want those privileges or not, and regardless of their stated intent. Privilege does not assume a life of ease and comfort; it is a statement of fact, rather than a label or a judgement.

Unlike Black people, white people are frequently unaware that they are members of the dominant group due to the privilege of being able to see themselves as persons rather than as stereotypes.

There are things white people can do, say and experience that Black people cannot, purely to do with skin colour and where we are positioned in society.

Prejudice

A judgment or opinion that is formed on insufficient grounds before facts are known or in disregard of facts that contradict it.

Racism

A belief that Black people are inferior due to their skin colour and where that belief is baked into the fabric of society and systemised to create consistent favourable outcomes for some and consistent unfavourable outcomes for others.

If you've read this far, it's unlikely this is your belief.

White people freeze in horror if accused of racism, 'But I'm not racist, I don't think I'm superior' is a familiar knee-jerk response. For a white person to be thought racist carries unwanted baggage beyond a dictionary definition. Even the thought of it may feel like relegation to a special category of evil, created expressly for the worst offenders against humanity. And this reaction is not because they are overtly racist per se and have been 'found out'; rather the assertion is received as a personal attack on individual character or nature. But white people can be racist and play roles within racist systems without their individual character and actions being intentionally and consciously racist. Racism goes beyond that of individual (or overt) belief.

Individual (overt) racism

The beliefs, attitudes and actions of individuals that support or perpetuate racism in conscious and unconscious ways. Our cultural narrative about racism typically focuses on this form of racism and fails to recognise systemic racism.

Cultural racism

Views, opinions, stereotypes and 'truisms' that are built and perpetuated by the media in all of its forms. How we view people who are different than we are when we do not have direct exposure to them is heavily influenced by what is portrayed in the media.

For example, in horror films in the 1990s and 2000s, it was common to have only one Black character. And if they lasted beyond the first 15 minutes without getting killed off, they were doing pretty well!

Unless films or TV shows were catering to a Black audience, again there was usually only one Black character, who generally played a secondary role to the white lead. The TV series *Friends* is a great example. Despite filming over 236 episodes, this story of a fictitious group of friends living and working in New York City included only two main Black characters, and the comedic punchlines were usually steeped in racial stereotypes.

Institutional racism

Occurs in an organization. These are discriminatory treatments, unfair policies or biased practices based on race that result in inequitable outcomes for white colleagues over Black colleagues, and extend considerably beyond prejudice.

It is a collective failure to provide appropriate support to people because of their skin colour and it manifests itself within processes, procedures, attitudes and behaviours and assumes formally or informally that Black people should be subordinate to white people.

> *I've never had a Black manager before and I wasn't too sure what to expect.*
>
> LinkedIn comment, 2021

Internalised racism (oppressor and the oppressed)

The process whereby Black people make oppression internal and personal by coming to believe that the lies, prejudices and stereotypes about them are true. Black people exhibit internalised oppression when we alter our attitudes, behaviours, speech and self-confidence to reflect the stereotypes and norms of white people. Internalised oppression can create low self-esteem, self-doubt and even self-loathing. It can also be projected outward as fear, criticism and distrust of other Black people.

Even as a victim of racism because of ethnicity, a Black person with power and influence can be an oppressor as we don't dismantle the systems and the barriers that other Black colleagues are facing. This leads to the maintenance of the status quo and the conservation of power, not through privilege but through the requirement of safety and the prestige, status and rewards that come through proximity to white people in positions of power.

If you're the only Black person on a board, you're not safe, and it is not safe for you to petition of behalf of your Black colleagues because you can lose your position to the majority (i.e. white people). As the only Black person on a board, in a team, in an organization, you have learnt to play the game, sometimes at a cost of your well-being, identity and ability to overtly challenge racist and discriminatory behaviour to which you are subjected.

We call it turning the other cheek.

Systemic (covert) racism

The way our society and the institutions within it are structured and replicated, and the ways people act and interact within them. This can include criminal justice systems, political power, social support and health care, but also unquestioned social systems. And within those social systems, systemic racism is harder for white people to identify because these systems assume white superiority individually, ideologically and institutionally. White people may not see themselves as overtly racist, but they still benefit from a social system that privileges white faces, voices and names.

To recognise and acknowledge this truth – that our entire societal structure maintains an oppressive system that privileges white people and oppresses Black people – carries great weight. It requires white people to see a large part of society in painful terms. It questions our humanity and our ingrained belief that our society is fair, tolerant and equitable. And it forces us to recognise the undeniable reality of white privilege.

And before you ask. . .can Black people be racist?
No.

To be racist requires benefiting from a systemic supremacy inherent in obtaining and maintaining societal, political and economic power and privilege. A person of any race can have prejudices about people of other races, but only members of the dominant social group – white people – can exhibit racism because racism is prejudice plus the institutional power to enforce it.

Social Capital

The shared norms, values and understandings that facilitate co-operation within or among groups.

The power of a CEO and, in smaller teams, workplace leaders is in their ability to generate social capital. They have a high level of control over cultural norms and procedural rules within organizations making them. Social mobility depends on access to resource rich social networks (e.g. money, advice, job referrals, mentorship programmes). The adage 'it's not what you know but who you know' rings true.

Because high-level colleagues are generally white, this creates racial boundaries around networks of opportunity that in turn create a white hegemony within workplaces.

Stakeholder Capitalism

Where organizations serve the interests of all their stake-holders (e.g. customers, suppliers, colleagues, shareholders, local communities). Under this system, a company's purpose is to create long-term value and not to maximise profits and enhance shareholder value at the cost of other stakeholder groups.

See also **Equity and Equality; Human Capital; Individualism; Meritocracy; Sustainable.**

Stereotype

An exaggerated or distorted belief that attributes character-istics to Black people, simplistically lumping them together and refusing to acknowledge differences among them.

Sustainable

The effect an organization has on society, to the extent that it views itself as a member of society and promotes business values that respect human capital. Such organizations mon-itor the impact of their operations to ensure that their short-term profits do not turn into long-term liabilities.

Board executives are often reluctant to make sustaina-bility core to their company's business strategy in the mis-taken belief that the costs outweigh the benefits. On the contrary, academic research and business experience point to the opposite.

Sustainable businesses redefine their corporate ecosys-tem by designing models that create value for all stakehold-ers, not just a 'green' agenda.

See also **Equity and Equality; Human Capital; Individualism; Meritocracy; Stakeholder Capitalism.**

Tokenism

A forced form of diversity that creates a superficial impression of equality without achieving it. It's the practice of making a symbolic action by recruiting a small number of Black people to create an appearance of racial equality.

If you're thinking, 'How much diversity in the workplace is needed to avoid tokenism?' you're asking the wrong question.

Tone Policing

Dictating how Black people should speak about racism and their lived experiences, with the objective of having Black people speak in a way that is acceptable to white people and doesn't cause them undue harm or distress.

White Backlash

A counter reaction by white people that produces a politics of displacement, shifting focus from Black people who are denied workplace equity to white people who imagine a threat or inconvenience in the possibility of workplace change through the advancing of racial equity.

> *I actually think that white people are being discriminated against. We mustn't forget that white people aren't the enemies. It's now harder for me as a white man to get a job because being white is now out of fashion.*
> LinkedIn comment, 2020

White Fragility

Feelings of discomfort a white person experiences when witnessing discussions around racial inequality and injustice.

For example, Black people may find it difficult to speak to white people about white privilege and superiority because a white person may become defensive and a Black person may feel obligated to comfort the white person because we live in a white-dominated environment.

When Black people discuss racism, white people may react in certain ways, including anger, fear, guilt, arguing, silence and/or leaving the situation. By behaving in this way, white people may prevent Black people from attempting to talk about racism with them.

White people may experience racial stress from various sources:

- A person claiming that a white person's views are racist
- A Black person talking about their racial experiences and perspectives
- A Black person not protecting a white person's feelings about racism
- A fellow white person not agreeing with another white person's perspectives on racism
- A white person receiving feedback that their behaviour or actions had a racist impact
- A white person being presented with a Black person in a position of leadership

Other triggers of white fragility may include situations wherein white people are not central. For example, white fragility may occur when watching a movie where a Black person is driving the story's action or is in a non-stereotypical role, or when there is a feeling that diversity has gone too far with the number of Black people portrayed in adverts or in television shows.

White people may not be overtly racist, but experiencing white fragility can contribute to racism. White people defending themselves or arguing against white superiority prevents conscious discussions with Black people about race and racism.

White Privilege

Refers to the fact that white people have advantages in society that Black people do not.

See also **Power, Rank and Privilege** on page 98.

White Saviour (White Saviourism)

White saviours often speak passionately about their desire to 'do the right thing'. Yet their actions usually involve very little input from the people they're attempting to help. Their intentions may be noble — many white saviours believe their actions challenge white supremacy and support the dismantling of racism.

In reality, though, white saviourism tends to emphasise inequality, because it continues to centre the actions of white people while ignoring (or even invalidating) the experiences of those they're claiming to help.

White saviours may be keen to be where all the action is – such as join in on conversations with Black people – but are reluctant to challenge their friends, family, peers and acquaintances, particularly if they are on their own or there isn't the opportunity for others to witness their challenge.

See also **Performative Allyship**.

White Supremacy

The belief that people with white skin are superior.

Whitewashing

A process that denies race and superimposes white culture. In business it is the purpose, method and result of radicalising the workplace as white. Just as the purpose of whitewashing a wall is to 'wash away' undesired markings, the purpose of whitewashing the workplace is to 'wash away' undesired racial politics.

> *The method chosen to 'wash' a wall is to cover the markings with white paint; the method chosen to 'wash' the workplace is to deny that racial politics exist and to cover them with white culture. As an end result, just as the whitewashed wall is seen as clean even though it is covered in white paint, the whitewashed workplace is seen as colourless even though it is fully immersed in white culture. It is a pervasive camouflage that serves to naturalise racial dynamic in the workplace.*
>
> Reitman, 2006, p. 268

***

Black

For the majority of global history the world got along fine without racial terminology.

Before the 1500s the word 'race' was rarely used, and only then to identify groups of people with a family relationship. And before the mid-1600s, the era of the Enlightenment, there is no evidence to suggest that the English referred to themselves as white people, nor was there terminology to describe people in degrees of proximity to whiteness, nor were phrases such as BAME or BIPOC used as a way to 'other' people against the standard of whiteness.

The Meaning of Black

'Black' was a term given to Black people to differentiate them from white people in order to bolster the racist ideology of whiteness that began in the seventeenth century.

Black people never called themselves Black. We do now – some of us at least. But back then, we never used the term.

> *My eldest daughter was six years old when she realised she was Black. It wasn't because I taught her. In fact I never really referred to the colour of her skin until she came home from school upset because a child had referred to her as Black. She didn't like it and she told her teacher, who reiterated that my daughter was Black. But Mummy, I don't even look Black. I'm brown.*

My youngest daughter is bi-racial. I dread to think what her initiation into Blackness looks like. I'm confused when it comes to ticking the ethnicity box in government consensus forms.

This isn't about her nationality – British and Estonian – but about how she will be labelled by society and therefore how it impacts her identity and the way she is treated.

Black is a political term.

This doesn't mean you shouldn't use it. Please do. It refers those who are African or have African heritage and denotes a shared culture and identify. That's how many of us use it today. If you are unsure, ask. But as part of deconstructing language and labels, to understand the context of Black you need to understand the social constructs of white, and whiteness, because within the English language in its current portrayal, thanks to the Enlightenment, we only understand the political term 'Black' as it relates to 'white'. They were set in opposition to each other as an opposing dyad: Black/white.

If this is difficult to get your head round, think of it a different way. Consider the words 'France' and 'Botswana'. It is possible to understand France without knowledge of Botswana and vice versa. There is no inherent political value in setting a native or inhabitant of France against a native or inhabitant of Botswana; neither term carries meaning in relation to the other. A person from either can be appreciated for their individuality – their bad jokes, their pastimes, their charity work, their love of salted caramel ice cream and reality TV (particularly the ones about real estate).

Here are just two humans, one from France and one from Botswana, living their best lives distinguished by what makes them unique and interesting.

However, if one of these humans is a Black person and the other white, consciously and/or subconsciously white people begin to make decisions about the Black individual in relation to the Black person's proximity to whiteness – their personality, aptitude, social standing – before the Black person even has a chance to open their mouth to say 'hi'.

And here, for the Black person, the freedom that individuality affords ends. Their reality is reduced to the collective noun of Black. On the other hand, the white person maintains their individuality because, due to the power, rank and privilege white people possess, white is not considered to be a collection of humans taken as a whole. Socially and politically, white is not a collective or even an ethnicity.

A great introduction to understanding the political value of the Black/white dyad is the prison library scene in Spike Lee's film *Malcolm X* (1992), when John Bembry (Albert Hall) asks Malcolm X (Denzel Washington) if he's ever looked up the word 'black' in a dictionary:

                    DICTIONARY
Black, (blak), adj. Destitute of light, devoid
of color, enveloped in darkness. Hence, utterly
dismal or gloomy, as "the future looked black."

                  MALCOLM'S VOICE
You understand them words?

                  BEMBRY'S VOICE
Read it.

                    MALCOLM
I can't make out that shit.

                    BEMBRY
Soiled with dirt, foul; sullen, hostile,
forbidding -- as a black day. Foully or
outrageously wicked, as black cruelty.
Indicating disgrace, dishonor or culpability.

                    DICTIONARY
See also blackmail, blackball, blackguard.

                    MALCOLM
Hey, they's some shit, all right.

                    BEMBRY
Now look up "white."

Bembry turns the pages of the dictionary to "w."

                  BEMBRY (contd)
Read it.

```
MALCOLM'S VOICE
White (whit), adj. Of the color of pure snow;
reflecting all the rays of the spectrum. The
opposite of black, hence free from spot or
blemish; innocent, pure, without evil intent,
harmless. Honest, square-dealing, honorable.
```

Blackness is the antithesis of whiteness.

When free people first stepped into slave ships they went in as Igbo, Hausa, Yoruba, but came out as Black, an amalgamating term that decrees millions upon millions of people have a collective identity as chosen by white people.

My hope is that, at least in my children's lifetime, we will do away with Black as a political term and take back the idea that we can be from the countries of our origin or where/what we identify as. So Black people become like everyone else – French, Chinese, Spanish, African-Caribbean, Japanese – because at the moment Black people are like an island that is deliberately set up untethered to anywhere.

The Fear of Black

Why are 40% of UK's working professionals scared to say the word 'Black' in relation to race and ethnicity in the workplace? Does saying Black make you uncomfortable? Are you scared of saying it wrongly?

Think about this for a moment. If you are scared of saying Black, Black person, Black colleagues, Black people, Black board member, Black colleague, and you aren't going to say 'Black', what are you going to say instead?

BLACK

Face your fear of the word because if you need ten conversations to get to the point of being comfortable about saying

Black, it will take another five hundred years for racial equity to advance anywhere.

In fact, between the time I first had the idea to write this book and having it published, I continued to update my language. And even now, I have started to use African heritage to describe my identity. And I've stopped leading with my ethnicity, as a label, first.

However, just to be clear, it is okay to say the word 'Black'.

Colour Blindness

The ideology of colour blindness legitimises practices that maintain racial inequity. It enables white people to avoid addressing systemic racism in the workplace by denying the lived experiences of Black people.

If white people are not paying attention, if they are 'colourblind', they never have to question whether race is a factor in, for example, their hiring. It benefits them not to question why they got a job because it makes it look like they got to where they are in their career on their own. Failure to see and acknowledge racial differences makes it difficult to recognise the unconscious biases everyone has.

A Black person will never say 'I don't see colour' because our race and culture are not the centre of the universe. We do not have that privilege.

Capitalising the B

Capitalising the B in Black is the difference between a colour and a culture. But I do not capitalise white.

Before anyone steps to me with comments about fairness and reverse racism, recognise this: White is capitalised by hate groups.

And white people, generally, have less shared history and culture in the way that Black people do. They have the luxury of being seen as individuals. There is no collective sense of a white community; meanwhile, Black people are judged as a collective. Ring fenced. Unable to move out of the societal construction of Blackness that was forced upon us.

White people's questionable behaviour is excused as the result of one bad apple.

Black people are seen as monolithic. To see one is to see us all. And when we fail, make mistakes or commit wrongdoing, we are deemed to tarnish the whole race and reinforce the stereotypes and judgements that already exist.

> *I'm not sure if we're ready to have more Black people. I would, of course. But my boss had a bad experience with my predecessor and now is reluctant to give another Black person a shot. I know it's unfair, but better I tell you now so you don't waste your time recruiting someone who I know won't fit in.*
>
> Department head, 2021

And yes, whiteness operates racially but there is nothing equal about how it operates in relation to how Blackness does.

And yes, equating the terms might be grammatically correct, but racial issues are larger than grammar.

After the murder of George Floyd, publications on both sides of the Atlantic changed their style guides to capitalise the B in Black. The Associated Press has changed its influential writing style guide to capitalise the B when referring to people in a racial, ethnic or cultural context

(*Guardian*, 2020). The *New York Times* (Coleman, 2020) changed its terms of usage to 'better reflect a shared cultural identity' as did many other Universities, publishers and media outlets.

Whilst there might be legitimate arguments for the capitalisation of white from highly reputable sources, I've done my research and made my decision.

You need to do the same. And you need to keep your decisions under review as meanings change.

But if you stay curious, this won't be an issue. Saying the word 'Black' won't be an issue, nor will be your refusal to take a colourblind approach, because when we come from a place of curiosity, we think more deeply about decisions and come up with more creative solutions. We experiment, collaborate, inspire and trust.

And you acknowledge that your ignorance isn't a blocker to taking action. It just means you have to keep learning.

Like we all do.

This is how you advance racial equity in your work-place: through curiosity and a willingness to try.

Are you ready?

It's so difficult to work out what to do in those situations. Playing devil's advocate, it could be that they are just oversensitive because they are the only one. Don't you think there's a heightened aware-ness that means they can see things that actually aren't there? How is it possible that amongst all of our leaders, none of us have ever had an issue with Black people or seen anything that looks untoward. It's our word against theirs.

Company secretary, 2021

Colourism

Some of us in America, the West Indies and Africa, believe that the nearer we approach the white man in colour, the greater our social standing and privilege and that we should build up an "aristocracy" based upon caste of colour and not achievement in race.

Marcus Garvey, 1923

Colourism describes the value and privilege associated with the lightness of a person's skin colour. It is an issue in many global majority communities, yet within the Black community it is an internalised form of oppression. Colourism taps into the notion that the closer we look to white people, as depicted by the shade of our skin colour, the safer we'll be. This safety typically looks like elevated status, opportunities, acceptance above other darker-skinned Black people. It's an assumption by society, not just by white people, that lighter-skinned Black people are more desirable and more acceptable. Amongst my community, we refer to this as 'light skin privilege', the holding of some form of white privilege without actually being white.

Colourism is not separate from the systemic elements of racism, but to understand racism, you have to be aware of colourism. Where there is one, there is the presence of the other. It can be perpetuated by anyone, not just white people.

You need to ask yourself whether all of your new global majority hires are of a light complexion. Do they have greater vertical mobility? Are they compensated more through benefits or mentoring opportunities due to their close proximity to whiteness? To their proximity to the seventeenth century standard of the rational human? Does your organization operate a 'skin shade gradient' when it comes to pay (Goldsmith, Hamilton and Darity, 2007)? Are your colleagues with closer proximity to whiteness more likely to be listened to and accepted in meetings than their darker-skinned colleagues?

You need to have greater awareness of the nuances of colourism.

Proximity to Whiteness and Power

There are Black professionals who believe they are protected and insulated from racism because they hold very senior positions within their companies. In this context, proximity to whiteness is not only about physical appearance but how close someone is to the real seat of power: the boardroom.

A tool of systemic racism is how 'good behaviour' is rewarded by white leadership teams. Good behaviour means you don't disturb the status quo. Colleagues can challenge but not too much, and being overly vocal about racism and discrimination is punishable by exclusion, being labelled as a troublemaker, to lose the inherent privileges associated with your position and/or limit advancement and other career opportunities.

The discomfort in talking or doing anything about racism conditions us to toe the line. To stay silent. To wait for someone else to make the first move and table it as the 'any other business' agenda item.

In a workplace context, proximity to whiteness is a blessing and a curse for senior Black professionals. On one hand, the rank associated with seniority gets them into the leadership club, with the job title and the perks that come with it. They are accepted and seen as the exceptional Black person who has defied all the odds and 'made it'.

They are playing the game, not bringing race into the equation, and certainly not drawing attention to themselves in the context of their ethnicity or cultural heritage. And in some instances, they are also likely to engage in viewpoints that blame racial inequities on the lack of ambition, drive or focus of Black people themselves. Because look, they've made it, so why can't everyone else?

However, there is no such thing as true safety, because even in the highest corridors of power, Black people typically can't wield the power that their positions technically afford.

Turning the tide on Credit Suisse's profits, during what was a troubling period for many European banks, wasn't enough to protect Tidjane Thiam as Western banking's only Black chief executive.

> *Tidjane is a nice person, a great executive, but his 'flaw' is that he thinks the world is out to get him. He is too thin-skinned. He sees racism everywhere.*
> Individual involved in Credit Suisse board deliberations,
> *Financial Times*, 2020

As a Black CEO in a predominantly white industry, based in the predominantly white city of Zurich, Mr Thiam endured functions where colleagues dressed up and danced around in Afro wigs, sat through shareholder meetings where his background was called 'third world', and was berated in Switzerland's press for 'not being Swiss enough'.

> *This bank is called Suisse – Credit Suisse. I hear him [Mr Thiam] mention the third world – is that really what we want? That a good, solid, Swiss bank sinks to the level of the third world?*
> Credit Suisse shareholder, 2016

> *I hope he sent his money home. Then we can classify it as development aid.*
> Anonymous, *New York Times*, 2020

Three months prior to George Floyd's murder on the streets of Minneapolis, Credit Suisse's board of directors forced Mr Thiam to resign:

Even though three of Credit Suisse's top investors and several of its largest clients lobbied publicly and privately for Mr Thiam to remain

Even though an external inquiry unanimously concluded Mr Thiam knew nothing about the internal spying scandal that he was ousted over

Even though white CEOs within banking scandals have survived a lot worse, including market manipulating, internal and external spying, and having personal ties to Jeffrey Epstein

Even though he made a failing Swiss institution profitable, guiding it through one of its worst financial periods

Even though shares in the bank fell 5% on news of his departure

Even though Mr Thiam's replacement is deemed incapable by Credit Suisse's largest investors.

The board and media watched the bank being destroyed for 15 years, then they attacked the guy trying to clear it up.
Anonymous, *Financial Times*, 2020

I believe that there were a lot of articles fed to the Swiss-German press to make tensions rise and the situation untenable. . .it's like a parochial town rejecting a foreign body.
Anonymous Credit Suisse client, *Financial Times*, 2020

The illusion comes at a price.

Our presence is tolerated provided we don't bring undue attention to how our lived experiences impact on the way we see the world, our decision-making and when we, or others who look like us, call out wrongdoing. Proximity to whiteness can adversely impact our ability to bring our true authentic selves to work.

Professionalism is dictated by white norms and cultures, as evidenced by Western styles of dress, and the way Black people have to change their hairstyles to integrate into the workplace. Speech, communication style and accents are adopted in ways that ensure acceptance into the workplace. Yet this acceptance usually means foregoing culture, identity and norms – all to fit in.

A study conducted in Canada of job applicants with Asian names (names of Indian, Pakistani or Chinese origins) found that 28% were less likely to get called for an interview, compared to applicants with Anglo names, even if their qualifications were the same (Chen, 2017).

In the UK in 2019, a study conducted by Nuffield College Centre for Social Investigation found that global majority job applicants had to send 60% more applications to receive the same number of callbacks as white applicants (Centre for Social Investigation, 2019).

The psychological stress that comes with being the 'odd one out' is not something to be glossed over. Living and working within a racialised society means you spend more time evaluating the way you show up, how you interact with others, when to challenge and when to stay silent, because you are acutely aware of your precarious position. Added to that, you are conscious of the stereotypes and try extra hard to combat them.

If you do happen to have Black professionals who occupy senior roles within your organization, pause for a moment and think about what life is like for them. Reflect on your interactions. How often have you had a conversation about their experiences within the four walls of your company? How far are they able to speak truth to power? Will they be listened to? Or do you still believe all of this is a non-conversation?

***

We wanted the truth.
We wanted to know how Black colleagues felt. What barriers our organization presented that we weren't seeing.
We wanted to listen.
To do something but do it right.
But how?

Client, 2020

References

Centre for Social Investigation, Nuffield College. (18 January 2019). New CSI research reveals high levels of job discrimination faced by ethnic minorities in Britain. Retrieved 20 October 2021, from http://csi.nuff.ox.ac.uk/?p=1299.

Chen, Jenny. (23 February 2017). Asian Last Names Lead To Fewer Job Interviews, Still. Retrieved 20 October 2021, from https://www.npr.org/sections/codeswitch/2017/02/23/516823230/asian-last-names-lead-to-fewer-job-interviews-still?t=1633804902857&t=1634760932475.

Coleman, Nancy. (5 July 2020). Why We're Capitalizing Black. *New York Times.* Retrieved 6 January 2020 from https://www.nytimes.com/2020/07/05/insider/capitalized-black.html.

Credit Suisse reels as Tidjane Thiam exits the stage. (2020). Retrieved 20 October 2021, from https://www.ft.com/content/6a120b28-49ca-11ea-aeb3-955839e06441.

Ernst & Young. (2021). Targets bring more women on boards, but they still don't reach the top. Retrieved 14 September 2021, from https://www.ey.com/en_uk/news/2020/09/targets-bring-more-women-on-boards-but-they-still-dont-reach-the-top.

Goldsmith, Arthur, Hamilton, Darrick, and Darity, William. (September 2007). From Dark to Light: Skin Color and Wages Among African-Americans. *Journal of Human Resources* 42(4): 701–738. doi: 10.3368/jhr.xlii.4.701.

Guardian. (20 June 2020). Associated Press changes influential style guide to capitalize 'Black'. Retrieved 6 January 2022 from https://www.theguardian.com/media/2020/jun/20/associated-press-style-guide-capitalize-black.

Kelly, Kate. (3 October 2020). The Short Tenure and Abrupt Ouster of Banking's Sole Black C.E.O. Retrieved 20 October 2021, from https://www.nytimes.com/2020/10/03/business/tidjane-thiam-credit-suisse.html.

Oddlikeeeveryoneelse (2021). Retrieved 14 September 2021, from https://www.reddit.com/r/AskReddit/comments/j6b5pp/serious_white_people_who_grew_up_in_lowincome/.

Patel, S. (24 September 2020). Targets bring more women on boards, but they still don't reach the top. Retrieved 14 September 2021, from https://www.ey.com/en_uk/news/2020/09/targets-bring-more-women-on-boards-but-they-still-dont-reach-the-top.

Reitman, Meredith. (2006). Uncovering the white place: whitewashing at work. *Social & Cultural Geography* 7(2): 267–282. doi: 10.1080/14649360600600692.

YMCA. (29 October 2020). Young, discriminated, and Black: the true colour of institutional racism in the UK. Retrieved 14 September 2021, from https://www.ymca.org.uk/press-statements/young-discriminated-and-black.

Young, discriminated, and Black: the true colour of institutional racism in the UK (2021). Retrieved 14 September 2021, from https://www.ymca.org.uk/press-statements/young-discriminated-and-black.

Starting from Where You Stand

You can't fix what you don't understand. Jumping in with half-baked ideas or co-opting your current D&I activities and tweaking them to fit doesn't work. Speak to the companies who did just that and you'll find they discovered that it made little to no difference.

Exploiting diversity and employing more Black people does not show either yourself or your organization to be anti-racist. It does not enable inclusion. And it doesn't mean you don't have a problem with systemic racism.

This is the crux of the matter, and this is why I wrote this book.

The Easy Solutions Are Rarely the Right Ones

Representation – more Black people – has no correlation with the presence or lack thereof of racism. Nor does the sudden proliferation of Black people smiling on corporate websites and brochures, or leading anti-racism commitments with quotas and targets.

> *We want our company to reflect the communities we serve.*
> *Inclusion is important to us.*

These tropes have been used for decades and yet this has never translated into actual action, not really. You can still work in a corporate office in London or many other large cities and see only a handful of Black people in senior positions. If they're there at all, they tend to be concentrated in front-line operational roles, applying for internal roles and getting nowhere whilst at the same time watching their peers leap to new and different roles with dizzying frequency.

There are also companies who claim they have nailed diversity. Boasting about the number of different nationalities on their roster, they wield their HR database like a badge of honour.

It's great when you can run a list of all the different countries your colleagues hail from. But how many Black people do you have in your company? Where are they? What positions do they hold? How much influence do they have? What is the size of the budgets they command or the profit and loss accounts they are responsible for?

> *We have a challenge with the way we do succession planning.*

Yes you do, but only as it applies to your Black colleagues. Disabled colleagues. Women. The list goes on. Anyone who isn't white and male, if we're honest.

Somehow along the way, corporate executives confused representation with racism. They believed that the way to demonstrate they were serious about taking action was to hire more Black people. They briefed their recruitment teams with a specific mandate:

Find me more Black people.

Anyone with a picture on LinkedIn showing their ethnicity was likely to be deluged with profile views from headhunters or InMail messages asking if they'd be open to new roles.

Black is trending. Kind of.

C-suite executives proclaim loudly and proudly how many Black people they've hired last quarter and how very few white men made the cut. Not the best way to demonstrate a commitment to anti-racism and equity, but this was a common approach.

At the height of the Black Lives Matter movement, my colleagues and I reviewed over one thousand corporate diversity and inclusion statements and anti-racism commitments. The majority of them emphasised the need to recruit and retain more Black people, as the first commitment or action they would take. Two years on, as we spent time pouring over public disclosures from FTSE250 companies, we realised that not much had changed.

Not too many of them spoke specifically about the how, nor what they would do to address how racism and racial discrimination show up in their business.

'Diversity and inclusion' sounds so much nicer, softer than racism. But they don't mean the same thing.

I would like you to hold this one key thought in your mind: *There is absolutely no correlation between increased numbers of Black colleagues and a decrease in the existence of racism and racial discrimination.*

This is a particularly important point, and reduces the chance of you taking a binary approach when responding to increasing shareholder (in some cases), stakeholder and regulatory pressure to diversify your board and take diversity and inclusion seriously.

A Corporate Risk Issue

Legal & General, an investment manager with £1.2 trillion under management (Makortoff, 2020), warned FTSE 100 and S&P 500 companies that it will use its voting power against those failing to diversify leadership teams. The investment consequences of such a mandate from an asset manager holding at any one time a 2%–3% stake of most FTSE100 companies has the potential to impact whole industries, and due to the trickle-down effect of market forces, smaller and non-listed firms are likely to be caught in any aftermath.

And it's not just investment companies that require transformative change. The US Securities and Exchange Commission said yes to a proposal from NASDAQ in 2021 to implement a NASDAQ Board Diversity Rule. This requires companies listed on their US exchange to:

- Publicly disclose board-level diversity statistics using a standardised template
- Have or explain why they do not have at least two 'diverse' directors

British financial regulator the Financial Conduct Authority (FCA) is clamping down on firms with poor employee diversity across all internal teams (Financial Conduct Authority, 2021). And the FCA have gone further by requiring financial companies to create, and commit to, credible decisive plans to address social issues and climate change, demonstrating that surface-level tokenism is no longer enough. Companies have to go deeper, even if on the surface it looks like appointing a few more Black people is enough to demonstrate compliance.

And it must go much deeper still, because institutional investors and regulators are not the sole drivers of change. The convergence between businesses, investors, shareholders, suppliers, colleagues, regulators and customers is already apparent.

When, on 20 April 2021, former Minneapolis police officer Derek Chauvin was found guilty of murdering George Floyd, corporate America – the embodiment of the American Dream – spoke out collectively for the first time, and rallied behind the continued fight against systemic racism, for US social justice and police reform (Repko, 2021):

> *There are countless examples of violence against Black men and women that don't end this way. In the past year, a number of brutal and senseless murders of Black Americans – from Ahmaud Arbery and Breonna Taylor to Daunte Wright and many others – remind us of the stark reality and persistence of systemic racism in our country. They sparked anger, awareness and dialogue; but not the change needed to address injustice in our communities and institutions. As an airline, we bring people of all races, ethnicities and backgrounds together every day.*
>
> *We believe Black lives matter. We know there is more work to do to achieve racial justice and equity in our society, and we remain committed to the journey.*
>
> – Excerpts from a letter sent to colleagues Tuesday night [20 April 2021] by American Airlines executives, CEO Doug Parker, President Robert Isom and Cedric Rockamore, vice president of global people operations and diversity and inclusion.

We are hopeful today's verdict will allow a grieving family and a community to start to heal. However, the systemic racism and social injustice apparent in the killing of George Floyd and countless other terrible episodes in our country are deeply rooted. Together, we must remain thoughtful and determined in addressing this reality, including the unacceptable abuse of authority and power and the pain it causes – disproportionately for the Black community and other people of color. For our part, Ford and our UAW partners will continue to create a company culture where everyone feels they belong and our differences are truly valued.
> – Bill Ford, executive chairman of Ford, and Jim Farley, CEO, said in a statement

Justice was served, it's the beginning of a long path to fix some of these things. We haven't solved this racial inequality problem for hundreds of years, and in fact in some decades it's gone backwards.
> – Jamie Dimon, JPMorgan Chase CEO, said Wednesday [21 April 2021] at a company event

But let's not pretend this is justice (H/T @deray) – And let's not forget to keep sending the message that our work is not done.
> – Jeff Lawson, co-founder and CEO of Twilio, said on his personal Twitter account

Corporate America decided that the risk of saying nothing, for not getting involved, was too great. That speaking out against systemic racism and racial inequity within the US social justice system was better for business.

Let's take a moment here, because this is a sea change in collective corporate direction, a recognition that 'business as usual' is a business model for failure. It is a demonstration of immense clarity that organizations with business plans projecting longevity are being cornered by stakeholders into fully comprehending what it means to have corporate responsibility: to plan beyond profit towards mitigating impact on the planet and to consider their role in solving society's biggest problems.

They are not relying on a casual tweets or blanket stand-in-solidarity hashtags and adverts. Irrespective of your personal thoughts about racism, the question you need to ask yourself is this: *What is doing nothing worth to my business, when customers, suppliers, regulators, investors and colleagues are no longer accepting the status quo that values ingrained false hierarchies of human worth?*

At this point, it would be remiss of me not to point out that not every organization is going to embark on this journey from a moral standpoint. There are leaders out there who genuinely couldn't care less about making a real difference for their Black colleagues, but they do care about how their company is perceived, about access to funding and about ensuring they don't find themselves in the middle of a race relations PR nightmare.

Anti-racism and advancing racial equity are tools to stay relevant. It's disappointing, yet it doesn't stop me from doing all I can to effect change. And it shouldn't stop you either.

So, assuming your company is planning for longevity, how far are you comfortable with your current plans to readdress racism: the inequities and inequalities that play out in your workplace and society as a whole?

Welcome to the global race to racial equality. And make no mistake – it is global, a worldwide issue, not one just connected to the West due to imperialism, colonialism and chattel slavery.

Equality is the destination. Equity is the vehicle to get us there.

So Now What?

We're getting close to the moment of truth, when you need to decide, pragmatically, if you've got the moral courage, humility and tenacity to lead this change.

It isn't just about resurrecting conversations that may have gone a little stale, but about taking action. You need to assess your state of readiness even to start your organization's journey into advancing racial equity.

Just reading one or two books doesn't make you an expert. Just because your best friend's cousin works in D&I doesn't mean they have it all figured out either.

If you jump into this from a state of panic or crisis mode, without having the chance to talk to someone objectively, if you haven't validated or challenged your own assumptions, you can perpetuate more harm, safe in the knowledge that the impact on you as individual, your career, your life is negligible.

That is not true for your Black colleagues. Hasty, thoughtless actions will keep the wheels of systemic racism turning, despite your best intentions.

So even if every instinct you have is telling you to 'just start doing something', to jump in with both metaphorical feet – please don't. That approach can make things worse. To begin with, you need to understand racism as a system beyond behaviour, even those within instances of overt workplace racism, and to understand why belief and policies are geared towards supporting a perpetrator arguing, 'but I didn't mean it!' rather than a Black employee's distress in receiving, and then reporting, racist abuse. You will never be (and should never try to be) an expert on Black people, yet centring the people you're trying to make a difference for is fundamental to your progress.

This may be hard to digest, but confronting racism is not about the needs and feelings of white people. It's not about making yourself a hero or fleshing out some great PR for your organization. It's not even about just giving Black people a seat at the table. It's about removing the barriers that stop Black people from having a seat at the table, and then handing them a microphone. Building *with* them, not *for* them. Listening, empowering and experimenting. Constructing continuous feedback loops and keeping this on the agenda even when you're fatigued and wish this would all go away. This is what centring Black colleagues means. It is the difference between equality and equity, between good intention and transformative change.

So ask yourself, 'How do I currently show up for Black colleagues?' and 'How will I know if what we're doing is making a difference?' What are our measures of impact (not success) and according to whom? Are conversations about racism normalised, and if not, why has this never been approached within our organization? What do we currently do to retain, value and ensure the success of our Black colleagues? Is what we're doing enough?

Have we prioritised our Black colleagues? Or are we still not ready to do that?

These are tough questions. If you find yourself looking for a multiple-choice option, you're not alone. These questions can be challenging, depending on your starting point, the culture you have, the collective appetite for change and historically how far you've leaned into this conversations.

It's possible you don't have the answers straight away. You may need to do some introspective work and some research. Talk to a few people who challenge your thinking, as opposed to telling you what you want to hear.

That's okay. In fact, that's great, because it means you're curious to find answers and work towards solutions. But don't take too long or use this as an opportunity to procrastinate. The steps needed to begin to evolve your cultures are not linear or sequential. You will make continual tradeoffs between setting your strategy and action plans against experimentation and refinement.

> *I even went as far to change my name just to make white people more comfortable.*
>
> Client employee, 2020

> *Young Black people worry about employment bias, in particular that prospective employers will have a negative perception of them because of their name. Almost half (47%) of young Black people with experience of applications expressed that they felt the need to change their name when doing so. This suggests that they are aware that there could be prejudice based on ethnicity when looking for work.*
>
> YMCA, 2020

The Four Levels of the Racial Equity Maturity Model

'Can you give us some examples of who is getting it right?'

No matter how many times I give a keynote, present to an executive team or even have lunch with a CEO, this question comes up time and time again. Whether it's inherent competition or just the need to be reassured that another organization is going through the process and has come out the other side, every leader wants me to reel off a list of companies who are getting it right.

I rarely name organizations who get top grades, despite how often I'm asked. This is partly because I believe we should be looking to elicit feedback from colleagues – they are the true barometer of what's changed – and also because it becomes the kiss of death. For every brand that I might publicly give a shout out to, the next day there's bound to be something in the press that highlights all that glitters isn't gold. It's to be expected that no organization gets it right all of the time and every company has skeletons in their closet; to pretend otherwise is disingenuous.

There is no shortcut to doing this work. There is really no blueprint or playbook. And even if there were, you must be ready and willing to start the meaningful process of change, knowing that you may need to see the real impact in your tenure, possibly in our lifetime. A problem that has existed for centuries is not going to magically fix itself overnight.

However, I do appreciate the need to benchmark, to understand where you are and what good looks like. Based on the work my team and I have done with clients all over the world, we created a maturity model with four steps to help leadership teams evaluate their approach as it stands and what level they aspire to reach.

Anti-racism is probably one of the few business areas where most leaders don't want to be at the top. That feels far too radical!

Like any maturity model, ours serves to help our clients determine not only where they are, but where they want to get to and to help them make informed decisions about what that needs to look like along the way. There are four levels to our maturity model:

- Level One: A Compliance Issue
- Level Two: Intent to Be Inclusive
- Level Three: Strategic Focus and Specific Commitment
- Level Four: Public + Private Accountability

Level One: A Compliance Issue

Not everyone wants to start at Level One, seemingly the very bottom of the ladder, but it has to exist because if you're a Level One organization, leader or executive team, that means you take a compliance approach to racial equity.

Within your organization's policies and procedures you may have statements about racism, but how you show up is driven by policy. So you talk about having a zero-tolerance approach, but people need to refer to, say, page nine of your employee handbook to see what that is. There's a reluctance to talk about racism in the workplace, and when you do it is likely as a means to mitigate risk. Intentionally you may reach for what is considered 'low-hanging fruit', such as bringing in an unconscious bias trainer for half a day's training to repeat every two years.

If this is your approach in addressing racism, you'll deal with it only if racism becomes an issue, such as an employee discrimination case. And even then, it will be hush-hush and possibly with a mandate to 'make it all go away.'

You'll be questioning whether you can get away with doing nothing, hoping that this is an extended storm in the teacup and that people will turn their attention to other things. Or you may be making excuses about why action isn't feasible at this particular moment.

There will be no proactivity to advance racial equity in the workplace, and your board are nervous about anything that could be deemed risky. Also, the fact that you have few to no Black colleagues makes you wonder whether you need to do anything more than what you're already doing.

If you're at this stage, the bold and courageous steps you need to take will look a little different. Bold for you could be anything from having the conversation to not stuttering over the word 'Black' or wincing at the thought at having to talk about racism and racial equity. In public. With no notes. Or a teleprompter.

At Level One, considering public statements to the press or publishing your D&I report is not a viable option. It's the equivalent of going from zero to a hundred.

There is a lot of work to do here, because you and your executive team do not yet possess even the appropriate language to have the necessary conversations. So it's not so much a matter of saying 'don't go there', but you've got to be honest and recognise that having taken a compliance approach historically, using policies and procedures to do nothing more than mitigate legal risk is not role-modelling the right leadership behaviour to dismantle racism.

Your starting point is different than that of organizations further on in their journey. There is some work for you to do here also, to achieve the bold leadership required to lean into very uncomfortable conversations about race. You need to recalibrate how you are able to show up, and the level of commitment you are willing (and able) to make. It is likely that you work within quite a risk-averse culture, traditional industries that have been in existence for decades if not centuries, so this is going to be uncharted territory for your organization and quite possibly for you. It is going to push people to the edge of their comfort zone and beyond, but if you still hold tight to the idea that racism is nothing more than a compliance issue to mitigate legal risk, you're only going to make tiny incremental gains. And such gains only reinforce your compliance approach to racial equity.

One of the reasons for the Racial Equity Maturity Model is that people considering this journey need to be intentional with their decisions, and sometimes being intentional means that you have to be honest and recognise that your starting point may not be as advanced as everyone else's, or as advanced as you would like. This is fine. It will just have a direct impact on some of the steps you need to take, rather than the steps you would like to take, to ensure that you and your organization look good.

So to recap, no one wants to be in the bottom level, purely concerned with reputational risk about what can be demonstrated through a tick-box approach; for example, have all colleagues carried out unconscious bias training (tick, they do it every two years); are policy statements are in place (tick); are policy statements updated (tick); and did someone remember to publish this on the website (tick)?

To an outsider looking in, your lack of action thus far may give the perception that your organization is not 100% sold on the true power of inclusion, equity and difference. There is work to be done.

Level One: Reflective Questions

- How do you recognise the organizational and individual behaviours that maintain racist practices in the workplace?
- Are you confident that you understand the subtle ways in which systemic racism affects Black people?
- Why does dismantling racism and evolving your corporate culture matter?
- What is it about advancing racial equity that you are struggling with?
- How are you going to bring your teams on board with dismantling racism?
- How prepared are you to learn and do at the same time?

In a review once I was told that a couple of colleagues were 'scared of me'. I was baffled by this, so I pushed a bit deeper, asking why they thought that, what's your evidence etc. Turns out there had been no complaint, the issue hadn't even been raised by the colleagues in question. It was just 'a feeling' that my manager had. I was the only Black senior manager on the team.

Client Employee, 2020

Level Two: Intent to Be Inclusive

At Level Two there is a demonstrable attempt to be inclusive, so you don't need to be convinced about the power of inclusion. In fact, you often use phrases like 'We are committed to diversity and inclusion', and the murder of George Floyd encouraged you to renew those commitments, in a general sense.

You do deal with issues of racism and racial harassment, but probably in response to something happening rather than taking a proactive stance. It is unlikely that your organization is looking for ways to ensure your environment is set up to prevent racism and racial harassment from occurring in the first place. Everything will be geared around reaction rather than prevention.

Whilst you are committed to inclusion – and note that I don't use the word 'diversity' here – this could potentially be seen as something led by HR. You yourself might make this an HR-driven initiative, rather than a CEO- and executive-team-driven mandate. You might be quite generic in your language, so while you talk about diversity and inclusion, there is probably a reluctance to be specific, or to address specific groups within your workforce. For example, rather than mentioning Black colleagues, racism, anti-racism and racial equity, you might still be talking about making sure everyone belongs, so your language is very soft, very gentle and you may still refer to your Black colleagues under the umbrella terms of 'ethnic minorities' or 'BAME'. You are communicating your approach to inclusion but it probably follows standard rhythms and routines, such as during companywide engagement surveys, off the back of poll surveys or even as a response to something happening in wider society that you feel the organization has to say something about. Potentially what you're doing is affirming or reaffirming your organization's policy stance rather than getting into specifics about what you intentionally aim to achieve, and how you are going to go about it.

There is something else to think about if you are in Level Two. Advancing racial equity might be a case of 'Do as I say, not as I do'. You might be reluctant to address scenarios involving leadership behaviours perpetuating racism. Again, it is possible that not only are you pushing this agenda onto HR as their responsibility, but there is a case to argue that you are protecting others (for example, board members) from some of the things you are talking about that need to change, and/or you are shielding yourself from having to take responsibility for something you find uncomfortable to think and talk about. Advancing racial equity affects *everyone*, not just everyone apart from you and your executive board. You need to acknowledge that some discomfort may still remain when talking about dismantling racism with colleagues. Are you worried about being so specific that it exposes you as an organization? How do you feel about working through the discomfort?

These are some of the things you need to work through, and this is why there is a Level Two approach. Many people believe that an intent to be inclusive would ensure an organization's placement within a higher level, but the key word here is *intent*. There is not enough action. And this is the difference: although you are not treating racism as solely a compliance issue, and you have progressed from a Level One culture or leader, there is still nothing more than a generic intent, nothing specific about improving the lives of your Black colleagues and addressing some of the systemic racism within your workplace culture that you cannot see, because you're not ready to have a look. An umbrella concept for Level Two leaders and organizations might be that there is comfort with inclusion but discomfort in specifically talking about race.

There is intent to be inclusive, but this intent is driven mainly by HR. It's an 'HR thing', probably an individual within the team who also happens to be Black, or the HR team in entirety talking about racial equity but with radio silence from the board, except perhaps around annual

Level Two: Reflective Questions

- How do I start a conversation around race in the workplace, especially if colleagues and leaders are not comfortable talking about it?
- Why does my company work so well for people who look like me?
- What is it that makes people who look like me stay and Black colleagues leave?
- How do I engage with my peers and key stakeholders? Who is another person on the board who gets it?
- How can I let my teams know I'm serious and why it matters to me – not we (as in the executive board), but me personally?
- Where am I going to start to convert my intent into action?
- How far do my teams, HR and DEI leads have the knowledge and expertise to help me operationalize a plan of action?
- Do I know what I need? What I should be looking for?

statement time when reports need to be published and engagement surveys need to be rolled out. It is still driven by process, and with the HR team as custodians rather than the board, it's likely that no overarching strategy exists. Furthermore, even with a certain amount of intent, a Level Two organization uses very generic language – language designed so white people 'feel nice' that issues such as inclusion and belonging, 'ethnic minorities' and so on aren't so scary after all.

> *I also couldn't help but remember all the instances prior to George Floyd when I was the butt of 'harmless' Black jokes, when I brought up racial hardships and was met with awkward silence and sighs just short of an eye-roll, akin to 'this again!'.*
>
> Client employee, 2021

> *Young Black people explained that they experienced colleagues informing them that they were 'surprised that they have been promoted' and, in some cases, were told by other colleagues that they 'would not get a promotion' and to instead be 'grateful for the position of being employed in the first place'.*
>
> YMCA, 2020

Level Three: Strategic Focus + Specific Commitment

We're climbing higher up the maturity model to reach Level Three! If you have a Level Three organization, leadership or culture, that means you have strategic focus, and a specific commitment to inclusion that is driven by you and your board. HR may act as enablers of specific programmes to execute strategic plans or operational focus, but this is very much a 'you thing', not just in your language, the way you talk about your intentions to dismantle racism and become inclusive, but in the specifics about what you intend to do and what you are doing. Not your organization, not your board – this is very much your voice. And if you think this paragraph overuses the word 'specific', it's done deliberately to create the understanding that advancing racial equity is an identifiable personal mission of a Level Three leader. In Level Three you have moved out of the diversity and intention arena and into visible inclusion and transformative action.

A word of caution here, however. Whilst there is an emphasis on the word 'you', it doesn't mean you are the lone ranger, the only person driving change with everyone else passively looking on. It just means that you have taken up the mantle to take action. You've moved past ruminating over what you don't know, what you don't have at your disposal, and whilst you don't have all the answers, you care enough to commit your organization to embark on this journey.

What does this look like in an organization? Well, you'll be a little more proactive when it comes to race in that there are likely to be conversations happening. This is more than bringing in speakers to talk about racism. This is the fact that you have unlocked the ability for as many colleagues as possible to lean into such conversations. For example, you may have had a listening forum. You may have already committed to some sort of plan, or publicly expressed an aim or intent or an expression to do what you can to advance racial equity, and more importantly to eradicate racism. And you focus on eradicating racism in your company culture. Your language will be specific here; you have moved on from referring to your Black colleagues as 'ethnic minorities' or 'BAME'. You are now specifically speaking about Black colleagues. There is still some discomfort about 'What are we doing for everyone else?' or 'Are we doing too much? Have we edged too far into this?' particularly if you are focused on what competitors or peers in your industry or across other industries are doing. That's not so much holding you back, but raising question marks in your mind: 'If they're not interested in dismantling racism, should I be?' or perhaps 'They're doing just fine as a Level One or Level Two, so am I wasting resources?'

However, your colleagues will be aware of the company stance in this, not because they are all wholeheartedly in agreement with you, but because your intent is clear. It leaves no room for misunderstanding or confusion. Your personal standpoint takes the organization beyond what your policies and procedures say. At this level, you are also more likely to engage in public conversations about racism – your thoughts, perspectives, lessons learnt so far. You are, dare I say, okay with your discomfort because you see the bigger picture about what's at stake and why it matters.

Now there is some proactivity in addressing issues of racism and racial harassment in that you're not only having the conversation when something happens, but you are starting to get into some routine in communicating your approach with your colleagues. But it might just follow your traditional business cycle; for example, it might come off the back of an engagement or poll survey or because of something that happened in wider society. You may still wonder how often you should speak out on social justice issues. Does it look bad if I say nothing? Or do I look too eager if I say something?

This level sounds okay, you might be thinking. So what's the difference between Level Three and Level Four? What keeps leaders and organizations sitting in Level Three is their reluctance to address their own and board leadership language and behaviours. You need to consider what needs to be done differently in order to effect change, and also what behaviours are no longer acceptable. It's not just about what people do or don't say; it's also about addressing silence, about bystander behaviour, and about doing nothing in the face of discovering a colleague is being treated unfairly.

It means demonstrating consequences, and communicating that to reinforce the idea that your values aren't just words on your meeting room wall, but that you live and breathe them and hold all your teams to that standard.

If you haven't been as proactive about dealing with issues of racism within your company historically, you may still worry about how you can all of a sudden hold your leadership teams to account. You might still be thinking that, generally, you have 'very nice board members', and it worries you that you're abruptly going to demonstrate cancel culture by no longer condoning behaviours that you used to accept. So while it's applaudable that you're focused and committed, the key thing that is still missing is accountability; both public and private.

Level Three is where things become tangible. There is a strategic focus on specific commitments to racial equity. The agenda is being driven at board level. Here companies are likely to have a CEO who is vocal about anti-racism, even just internally: 'This is what I want us to commit to', 'This is how I want us to show what anti-racism means to the company' and so on. There's a lot of 'I' statements from the CEO rather than 'we'. The language is specific. And although the company is getting into its rhythms and routines with a racial equity plan, it's not 100% confident of its contents. The company is likely to struggle with external communication and what it should look like, and may feel on rocky ground when it comes to understanding when they should be speaking publicly about certain issues and when they should stay quiet. They may struggle to figure out when to reach out to their Black colleagues and when to wait for permission. You don't have all the answers, the resources aren't quite lined up, but there is a definite JFDI (*just f*&%ing do it*), about getting on with getting on.

Level Three: Reflective Questions

- How does your view on dismantling racism, and advancing racial equity in your organization, shape how you see and understand the role of your organization in being a force for good? What's holding you back from taking things to the next level, i.e. Level Four?

- Consider an issue in advancing racial equity within your organization – for example, executive board behaviour. How can you open the conversation and help your peers and direct reports understand what accountability looks like?

- What is your response to challenges from executive board members to dismantling racist language, microaggressions and behaviour?

- Do you know of other leaders advancing racial equity in their organizations? Could you reach out to them? Or can someone facilitate an introduction for you?

- Does dismantling racism seem possible within your organization? If so, why? If not, why not?

- How far is there energy and appetite to keep going? Is there still enthusiasm for action?

- Can you identify peers on your executive leadership team who feel just as strongly about this as you? Or do you feel alone? what can you do to change that?

- Who acts as your independent voice of challenge, to make sure you don't mark your own homework, so to speak? Who can you confide in? Who can you trust?

We need to fix ourselves internally before we can go public.

Client, 2020

Goldman Sachs is a perfect example. They announced that they're giving Black female entrepreneurs millions of dollars due to the effects of Covid-19 on Black female-owned businesses. And my first question was, after reading that, what are you doing for the Black women in your multi-billion-dollar company?

Dr. Janice Gassam Asare, anti-racism educator and DEI consultant, 2021

Level Four: Public + Private Accountability

l always smile when I talk about Level Four, the holy grail of the Racial Equity Maturity Model. It's a great level, but not everyone sees it as an aspirational destination. Why? Because public and private accountability means there's nowhere to hide. You have to see it through and you are held to a particular standard, which entails upholding your commitments, leading with authenticity instead of corporate spin, and being truthful about where you are and the impact of your initiatives and programs.

Personally, I feel disappointed that people opt out of striving to reach this maturity level. Professionally, I've learnt to accept it.

If you can help us get to Level Three, I'll be happy with that!

Chairman, 2021

Level Four means not only being able to walk tall, in that there is board ownership and accountability, but also that there are specific corporate plans in place to advance racial equity. The language is very specific and very intentional. You are communicating your approach to the external world. You have an anti-racism action plan and you will also expect your supply chain and the people you collaborate with to adhere to a standard, that they too are advancing racial equity within their organizations. You are setting expectations not only for your colleagues and executive board but also those who sit within your ecosystem and support you. You might go as far as requesting access to the inclusion reports or the anti-racism plans of your current and potential suppliers and partners. You are setting an expectation that says, 'If you want to work with us, this is what you will need to do as a bare minimum'. You are using your influence to effect change in your supply chain, with your partnerships and your collaborators, developing positive pressure to get more people to make change and commit to action. This means a Level Four leader/organization has a regular rhythm and routine of communication. There will be specific communications going out to colleagues and also regular communications going to investors and other stakeholders, and not just in a reactionary way on the back of an earnings call or because one of the investors has said, 'We need to see your plan'. There is a proactivity in Level Four that other levels and organizations don't have.

Yet there are some things to watch out for at this level.

Many leaders are tempted to overestimate how mature they are in this space, because they knee-jerked and rushed out statements and social media posts. They confuse the external communication as the ultimate destination, not recognising that there has to be substance behind the words. Their initiatives and the impact need to be verified, if not by an independent party, then at least by the employees who are most impacted by racism. Most decision makers get carried away with the slick brochures and the stylised employee talking head videos think style over substance.

Make sure you are centring and amplifying your Black colleagues. Guard against focusing on racial equity purely as an opportunity to 'show off' to your investors and stakeholders and then wind up overlooking your colleagues internally – both your Black colleagues and your other team members who have a crucial role to play in your transformation programme. Only by centring those most impacted can you guarantee that their experience in the workplace is significantly improved.

You need to sense-check now and again that you are giving enough energy and attention to internal independent reviews concerning the way you do things, both formally and informally, that potentially perpetuate racism. How much alignment is there between what you say you're doing versus how it feels for your Black colleagues? How far have you invested in creating a continuous feedback loop that is based on psychological safety? In other words, are you open to the observations and challenges posed by your colleagues, irrespective of their ethnicity? For both those who think you haven't done enough as well as others who feel you are doing too much, open dialogue is key.

At Level Four, the push for advancing racial equity is a business-led strategy, a strategic imperative. It's linked to your values. You've recalibrated your leadership traits to ensure the right behaviours are recruited for, developed and rewarded. There is specific language about race, racial equity and racism. There is commitment to inclusion and the different aspects involved. The company applies positive pressure on their suppliers and partners to do the same (i.e. for us to work with you we need to know your racial equity plan and your plan for gender representation). They get into specifics, and make decisions based on advancing racial equity. There is frequent, authentic internal and external communication. This is not tokenism akin to 'a few Black faces on a brochure' but an acknowledgement that there is distance to travel and hard work to be done, and that a strategic plan is being baked into the corporate culture, one that is measurable, decisive and open to being publicly challenged.

Which companies have attained Level Four status? No one has truly nailed it, but the key word here is 'authentic'. Level Four companies are those making proactive, authentic decisions: planning for racial equity within their walls and with their suppliers and external stakeholders, and using their power and privilege to advocate for greater change, greater transparency and holding their industry to account.

Level Four: Reflection Questions

- Can you think of an example where the external image of your organization does not reflect the internal workplace experience of your Black colleagues? How can this be changed?
- How do you ensure your organization's external image equates to internal workplace reality?
- How are your Black colleagues centred in your organization's roll-out of its equity plan? How do you ensure this stance is maintained?
- How much have you invested so far? What difference has it made to dismantling systemic racism and advancing racial equity?
- How are you supporting the colleagues who are operationalising the racial equity plan?
- How far is their clarity on the difference between anti-racism and racial equity? Are you confident your actions to date are still homing in on identifying and taking corrective action for dismantling systemic racism within your workplace?
- How are you sharing responsibility for execution and ensuring you are not relying on your Black colleagues to do the heavy lifting?
- What are your fears of maintaining your organization's course to advance racial equity? What are your hopes?
- What legacy would you like to leave behind, as an executive leader and an organization?
- Do you believe you can make it happen? If not, why not? And what can do you differently to make your vision a reality?

To sum up the Racial Equity Maturity Model:

Level One means you're treating racism as a compliance issue.

Level Two means there is intent to be inclusive. It's driven by HR with some pro-activity, but conversations are generic, and language is focused on diversity and inclusion rather than on racial equity, racism, Black colleagues and so on.

Level Three means there is strategic focus and specific commitment. Language is intentional and very clear. There is internal communication driven by the business or the board with a senior leader champion.

Level Four is Level Three with the addition of accountability, both public and private, with you leveraging your influence to effect positive change across your entire ecosystem.

> *When leadership is trying to make sense of someone who does something that is racist, it shouldn't matter if they're high performing or a high potential employee, if they're creating a toxic and hostile work environment. But oftentimes, leadership is very shortsighted and they're like, 'Well we'll keep this person because they're bringing us revenue and they have a huge ROI. . .it's okay if they're creating this toxic environment because they're counteracting that by their performance'.*
>
> Dr. Janice Gassam Asare, 2021

Our Culture Isn't Racist . . . Is It?

There is a distinct possibility you went into the Racial Equity Maturity Model thinking you and your organization were at least a Level Three, only to realise you're a Level

One. This happens a lot. It is one of the reasons why it is important to consider where you currently stand before jumping into action. If you think you're a Level Four but in reality you're pushing a Level Two *at the most*, then the conversations you are trying to engage in are beyond what your board and colleagues can currently cope with and will do more harm than good. And this is likely to build resentment quickly because you have failed to set firm foundations.

Yet don't lose hope.

When you're honest about your starting point and think you know where you stand but are still not 100% sure or don't trust yourself with your own conclusion, take the four-minute Equity and Inclusion Test (https://scorecard. hr-rewired.com/), which we use with anyone who comes to HR rewired for support. It's complimentary and it helps those with no idea what to do next. This at least provides conversation prompts to take back to your organization, along with this book, to help put a more structured approach into place.

Maybe you've realised that either you yourself and/or your company is currently at a Level One or Level Two, and your initial reaction is one of confusion or slightly defensive in nature, because you have the nicest board members; hire the best person for the job; and no one really says anything about racist behaviour, so how am I meant to know. . .oh, and you don't see colour.

But We Have Nice People. . .

As set out in Chapter 2, systemic racism is the foundation on which our society is built. To carry on with no active interruption of that system is to be complicit with it. This means that if you're not actively doing anything to dismantle racism besides being nice, you are complicit in the ideology's existence. There is no neutral territory with racism; you're either taking it apart or you're reinforcing it. Thus racism is not beholden to the words and actions of un-nice people, and niceness is not the answer to advancing racial equity. The fact that members of your white workforce volunteer for the local cat shelter, bring in homemade cake or haven't a bad word to say about anyone is immaterial. Yes, being nice is better than being mean, but it's not dismantling racism; it's not kindness, which is a form of compassion and will lead to creating action to support Black colleagues. Niceness is hollow and performative. Niceness is the deflection, the 'Oh, I didn't mean it' reaction to a microagression, rather than kindness, which sees the pain caused to others, the 'I'm sorry, I will do better and here's how' response. No organization needs nice people; you need kind people.

We Hire the Best Person for the Job. . .

Chapters 2 and 3 discussed meritocracy, but in case it didn't sink in the first two times: *Hiring the best person for the job is an elusive fantasy.*

What you do is hire the person who fits most closely with the image of what you want, given the amount of time you have to spend looking, the amount of resources you have to spend on the search, limited by the ability to test for the skills you think you need and by the set of people who will be attracted to work for you given your reputation and the job advert. This is not attracting the best person for the job. This is a historically proven format that attracts white people, because that is the image of what you want: someone like you, someone 'safe'.

Even if a few Black candidates get through to the interview stage, regardless of their ability your new employee will tend to look a lot like you. Because when faced with a set of candidates who each have the basic skills and experience to do the role, you end up hiring the one who makes you feel more comfortable, more confident. You go for safety. Even though you have read all the reports and seen all the statistics that say diverse teams are smarter teams, you hire someone like you.

If you conclude that your organization hires 'the best person for the job', dig deep into your hiring process to find out who it works for and why.

Nobody Really Said Anything, So How Are We Meant to Know. . .

If you've arrived at this conclusion, you're working from a Level One standing. Racism for your organization is a policy point.

Systemic racism is normalised throughout all of our societal systems. Even if you cannot see it – and you probably can't – it exists in your organization. Your Black colleagues don't talk about it because speaking truth to an ideology this powerful is risky. For a Black colleague to confront microaggressions or hold colleagues accountable for racism (whether overt or covert) means running the risk of harming their career, their social support network and their psychological well-being – all in relation to being honest about difficult issues. In speaking up, Black people risk being seen as biased, overly emotional (e.g. angry) and a whole host of other negative stereotypes that lie behind the problems we are addressing here.

There are reasons why nobody has really said anything. It's your responsibility to find out why.

I Don't See Colour. . .

After Chapter 3, there is a sincere hope that this is no longer your viewpoint. But let's extend understanding further.

As Black people, we are proud of our heritage, of what we accomplish knowing the backdrop of how society is wired. We want people to see us and to appreciate us because of our Blackness, not despite it. And colour blindness fundamentally misses the mark by erasing something that's fundamental to our identity and our self-love – and that's not the way to navigate through building an inclusive workplace.

Here at the end of Chapter 4 it is time to own the fight to dismantle racism in your organization. It is one that needs to be led by you and informed by your Black colleagues. And as you forge ahead, undertake the work outlined in the next chapter and recognise that it takes time. Dismantling racism is a process – for both you and your organization.

References

Financial Conduct Authority. (17 March 2021). Why diversity and inclusion are regulatory issues. Retrieved 19 May 2021, from https://www.fca.org.uk/news/speeches/why-diversity-and-inclusion-are-regulatory-issues.

Makortoff, Kalyeena. (5 October 2020). Legal & General warns FTSE 100 firms over lack of ethnic diversity. *Guardian*. Retrieved from https://www.theguardian.com/business/2020/oct/05/legal-and-general-warns-ftse-100-firms-lack-of-ethnic-diversity-bame-board-member-2022.

Repko, Melissa. (22 April 2021). After Chauvin verdict, business leaders speak out saying fight for racial justice must continue. Retrieved 19 May 2021, from https://www-cnbc-com.cdn.ampproject.org/c/s/ www.cnbc.com/amp/2021/04/21/chauvin-verdict-business-leaders-speak-out-on-fight-for-racial-justice.html.

The Four-Factor RACE Model

Our executive leaders live in white issues, 'none of this applies to me', 'where I live racism isn't an issue', etc. How do I break that stuff down without breaking people down?

Client, 2021

At the time of writing, only four Fortune 500 CEOs are Black. In the UK, there are no Black chairpeople, CEOs or CFOs in any of our top 100 largest companies as represented by the FTSE 100.

When diversity and inclusion statements are being compiled, the self-congratulatory note about what has been achieved so far should be taken with a grain of salt.

Whether or not we want to admit it, there is an assumption that senior Black executives do not have the skillset, the intellectual capability or the leadership ability to reach the highest corridors of power in the business world. The over-indexing on Black leadership development programmes is testament to that.

With the exception of diversity and inclusion roles (and even then, one could argue these roles have very little true influence and power to effect change), there is a reticence about putting Black people in senior roles that have real influence, power or substantive P&Ls to look after.

We're told we all have the same twenty-four hours in a day, and that if you work hard and apply yourself, those senior executive roles are yours for the taking. So, what do we do? We work even harder, feeling a drive to overperform and demonstrate a willingness and readiness to progress. We say yes to additional unpaid work in the hope it shows how truly committed we are. Yet even then we are overlooked. Or, when we are given the opportunities, these are the high-risk roles, the assignments that no one else really wants. That is also equally galling.

So how do we then, address systemic racism in the workplace, without the tokenism or performative gestures and statements?

Be Specific

In 2012 I was diagnosed with stage four Hodgkin's lymphoma. My diagnosis came almost too late for my treatment to make a difference.

I was misdiagnosed a number of times in the lead-up to finally finding out I had a big old tumor nestled within my chest. This misdiagnosis meant I spent time and money trying to alleviate the symptoms, never getting to the bottom of the cause, and making matters worse.

Stage four Hodgkin's lymphoma had made my life hell for the preceding fours month before being diagnosed by an incredible consultant, Dr Shafi, a specialist in hematology in Darent Valley Hospital in Kent. Hodgkin's lymphoma is a cancer of the blood and affects your lymphatic system. Like most medical issues, the diagnosis is just the beginning.

Dr Shafi subjected me to every test possible before I started treatment. He wanted to make sure he knew exactly where the cancer was showing up, before he prescribed either chemotherapy, radiotherapy or nothing.

It was frustrating at times, waiting for test results, having more blood taken, and being passed around different departments. I just wanted them to get a move on. I was tired, fed up, and after months of thinking that this was all in my head, the relief of being believed and feeling validated actually made me doubly impatient for treatment.

Yet for those who have experienced cancer, or have supported friends or loved ones with the diagnosis, you know that not every cancer is the same. The causes, the symptoms and the treatment differ and there are no guarantees that it won't ever come back again. Yet that didn't stop Dr Shafi and the multitude of other doctors and nurses doing everything they could, even if they couldn't predict a positive outcome. There were so many variables to take into consideration, so doing the investigative work was necessary to ensure that the treatment would have the best possible chance of doing what it was designed to do.

There were no debates about whether they should treat my cancer. No other consultant barged into Dr Shafi's office and demanded that he turn his attention to someone else. No other nurse complained that my tests were causing a backlog for other patients who had more serious symptoms than I had. The receptionist didn't argue that being specific about my cancer was being divisive. The cardiologist didn't chime in with 'What about *my* patients?' There was no expectation for me to educate anyone on Hodgkin's lymphoma. And Dr Shafi didn't gingerly tiptoe around naming my cancer. He was very open about the mortality rates, possible complications and such.

Honesty. Transparency. No debates about whether they should 'only' focus on my cancer. Instead, there was a commitment to do whatever they could, even knowing there were no guarantees.

Dr Shafi (a specialist) and the amazingly supportive doctors and nurses at the NHS (trained with a very specific expertise, in a specific type of cancer) are what I needed to save my life.

My GP at the time, Dr Bora, was great, but he is, by definition of his training and title, a general practitioner. He played a role, but it came much later, when I successfully responded to chemotherapy and the cancerous cells started to shrink. He was there to see how I was coping, that I was able to self-administer the drugs I was given to combat the side effects of chemotherapy and generally that the hospital was doing what they could to help. Dr Bora monitored my condition, offered a sympathetic ear when I needed it and took over administering my injections when I couldn't face doing it myself.

My cancer needed a specific intervention, a roster of individuals who offered more than empathy and a commitment to make a difference. It was a combination of specialist knowledge and general practitioner care rooted in action.

Racism needs specific intervention. Taking a generalised approach to specific problems never yields impressive results. Through no fault of his own, if my GP had tried to cure my cancer, I wouldn't still be here.

Once you understand where your company sits within the Racial Equity Maturity Model (see Chapter 4), you can consider how to approach dismantling systemic racism within your organization. I created a method to assist in this process: the Four-Factor RACE Model.

It's specific, transparent and gives you a framework to take substantive action on an ongoing basis. This model is codified from over 100,000 conversations unlocked about race, both individually and collectively within my advisory firm, HR rewired. It entailed conversations with corporates and startups; CEOs and HR leads; academics, politicians and legal teams; the military and various police forces; artists and creatives; regulators, social and health services personnel, including professional consultants across a vast array of industries; as well as some of the most prominent voices within anti-racism and racial equity. The participants came from across the globe, through keynotes, Zoom calls, listening forums, presentations and media interviews, in conversations to raise awareness and provoke others to act.

Combined with this, my team has reviewed thousands of corporate Black Lives Matter statements, anti-racist commitments and D&I reports to analyse where companies are in their journey, and whether their external image reflects their internal reality. There is no hiding the truth. I know what the hard work to dismantling racism looks like: the fears, the challenges facing companies who have already begun their journey. This is hard work, particularly if you're not used to having frequent open conversations about racism. It all comes down to your willingness for change and commitment to act, on an ongoing basis.

RACE is an acronym for **R**ecognise the problem, **A**nalyse the Impact, **C**ommit to Action and **E**mpower for Change, and the model was created to provide a framework to ensure the action you take is deliberate, intentional and impactful.

It is not a blueprint, a how-to or a step-by-step guide. It's also not a detailed list of every single action you could take. If I wrote this as such, by the time the ink has dried from the print run of the paperback version, some of what I've suggested might be out of date. It would also mean any plans you create are not yours, but mine or my company's. And that means no ownership or accountability.

Whilst the nuances of what constitutes good practice may change over time, I've written this book with longevity in mind.

> *The biggest part of the difficulty is that you feel that it cannot be discussed for fear of making people feel uncomfortable. I'm not one to keep my mouth shut by any means but the impact that has had on my life and career is hard to handle at times.*
>
> Client employee, 2020

Recognise the Problem

Chapter 4 may have revealed several uncomfortable truths about your relationship, and your organizations, with systemic racism. You may have a rough idea of the degree of introspection you and your executive teams are willing to do when it comes to the issues at hand, and you may possibly even recognise how prepared your company is to progress through the levels of the Racial Equity Maturity Model.

Chapter 4 gave some context to the knowledge that you cannot fix what you don't understand, meaning that you can't jump into 'solving' racism without getting clued into its insidious and often invisible presence in our lives. Yet the chapter also highlighted that starting from where you stand is not about becoming an expert in the Black experience, but is the basis to the beginning of your insightful journey of advancing racial equity. This starts with the questions the chapter asks of you, as a way to support your increased understanding of systemic racism and your part in dismantling it.

However, there is a second part to this knowledge, the fact that you can't solve what you don't talk about. This means you need to discuss the strategic imperative for change, the why behind these considerations: your move to amplify the voices of Black colleagues; your commitment to measurable action; understanding the language of what racism is; and what white privilege, white fragility and white supremacy mean and how they play out in your life. Without introspection and without understanding the why behind your need to advance racial equity, your effort will become tokenistic and can perpetuate harm. Do not simply jump into action; take some time.

This may feel a little repetitive, and has been covered in prior chapters. Yet it is vital to understand when taking appropriate action and ensuring your Black colleagues are not put in jeopardy by an ill-conceived anti-racist plan that falls flat before you've even got started.

Active Introspection

When considering the type of introspection that will form the basis of your words and actions to dismantle racism within your organization, begin by thinking about racism from your organization's perspective. Where's the pressure to change coming from? The influencing factors? Is it financially driven through growth into new markets? From investors or colleagues? Or indeed has the organization been too quiet for too long and now wants to catch up? The deeper you can take this, pushing past your discomfort to unearth the truth, the greater sustainable future change will be.

If you don't delve beyond the shallows for this first stage, nothing will change. Spend the time and turn the mirror on your organization.

Do you understand the current state of play, as it relates to the people most impacted by racism and those who promote, preserve and uphold the conditions that hold your Black colleagues back? What are your belief systems? The values that you need to question? Because if you're going to lead others to be introspective, then you've got to do the work yourself.

If your company is to have real conversations, and create physical and psychologically safe spaces to hear truths from Black colleagues about their life within your workplace – and not just those from the one or two Black colleagues whose stories are not particularly challenging to hear, because of their own personal reasons – then honesty is required.

What authentic reflections have you shared? Whose voices are you paying the most attention to? What stories do your wider workforce tell about the way their Black colleagues have been treated? Do you know? Or is that information blocked from getting to you? And if it does get through, would you care enough to do something about it?

If you don't have Black colleagues, then look to your parent company, supply chains, partners, investors or subsidiary companies. The introspection here works on the same principle; you're just broadening out.

The importance of this introspective analysis cannot be underestimated. Essentially, if the work isn't done, then your plan towards advancing racial equity is in performative territory. In order for your plan to succeed and make a difference, you and your organization have to move beyond the discomfort and recognise the problem.

> *I really want to do something about this but my boss just isn't interested. I know it shouldn't just fall on me, but I can't sit back and do nothing. That doesn't sit right with me.*
>
> Head of resourcing, 2021

Where to Start

You want to start with your executive team because if they have not bought into why advancing racial equity is important, that drastically decreases the odds of being able to do something meaningful in this space, no matter how committed you are to the cause. However, if you want to recalibrate people's knowledge on what racism is and what it isn't, you need to ask yourself as a leader about your personal feelings in this space, as well as the feelings of your board members. How do you view racism? How do your board members view racism?

This forms part of the active, ongoing introspection you are doing. This is not only to consider the change your organization could make, the level within the Maturity Model it might attain, but the beliefs and values you've held onto for the majority of your career, some of which have got you to this stage where you are leading an organization. You have to recognise there might be some things that you need to relearn, but also unlearn, to make sure you start your organization on an authentic journey in this space rather than project nothing more than a slick corporate presentation-style approach. This means you have to start with 'I' – for example, this is what I think, this is what I feel, this is what I've reflected on. And you want to encourage your executive board to go on the same introspective journey.

You also want to assess your organization's state of readiness to commit to dismantling racism, and this will be heavily influenced about what you've done historically, not just about racism but also your approach to inclusion and equity in general. Maybe your approach to thinking about difference amounts to nothing more than a consideration of people who are not white. Maybe diversity to you can be defined as nothing more than difference.

> *Working there was the closest I ever want to come to being on a plantation.*
>
> Client's employee, 2020

You cannot think that hiring a D&I consultant or a management consultancy company is enough on its own to fix systemic racism in your organization. They cannot do it *for* you. They can work in a vacuum if you have distanced yourself from the situation, but by staying out of the hard work you are saying that your personal feelings about systemic racism are not important. Yet they are, because your personal feelings, your convictions and the courage of your convictions, your values and your beliefs about whether you want to do this are what will sustain the course. Otherwise (and you already know this), any progress made will be over by the end of the financial year, or by the end of the second financial year. Dismantling systemic racism in the workplace isn't about a one- to three-year plan. It's not a problem that you're going to fix in the traditional sense. It is a slow but sure change toward putting impactful solutions into place, because you've decided as a CEO with the buy-in of your executive board that this is what your organization wants to do: how you are going to embed racial equity into business as usual, how it becomes part of your corporate DNA, how you show up. This is what you want to think about at this stage: Recognise the Problem.

So before you jump in and consider another external corporate communication, or contracting somebody to 'fix' systemic racism for you, have these honest conversations at board level to assist in helping you understand the individual issues your organization faces in tackling systemic racism within your company. But don't leap into solution mode yet without understanding the problem at hand.

You cannot fix what you don't understand, but also you cannot solve what you don't talk about. And the discomfort surrounding conversations about race and racism means that many people within your organization still don't understand the problem, or they believe it's just about behaviour.

I've had the 'aggressive' label levelled at me when a colleague made false statements in a meeting and I challenged her. Following the meeting I sent emails to all the meeting attendees with attachments proving her statements were incorrect. I got no acknowledgement of this from anyone, including the senior management who were in attendance.

Client's employee, 2021

You Don't Have to Be an Expert on the Black Experience

When you're doing the introspective work and raising your awareness of the issues your Black colleagues face in everyday life, it is easy for white leaders and white executive boards to focus too much on trying to become experts on the Black experience. And this is as relevant to the Recognise the Problem stage as it is to the other three steps of the RACE Model.

What this means is that all of the introspection, and eventually the insights and data, is driven to try and understand the barriers that hold back Black people from entering, staying and progressing within your organization. It's easier for leaders to spend time trying to understand what life is like for their Black colleagues. They ask questions, set up forums and so on, with the idea of exploring how to get deep into their psyche, believing that will demonstrate how these colleagues tick, how they think and what they expect.

Just to be crystal clear, you are working towards listening to and amplifying the voices of Black colleagues. I'm not saying you shouldn't do this. However, sometimes when you put so much energy and effort into trying to understand somebody else's experience in order for you to determine what you need to do differently, you miss one very important aspect of the work you're attempting to do: the ability to look at your own experiences.

Why does my experience differ so much from that of Black colleagues?

As a white person you know that fundamentally you cannot be an expert in the Black experience, but you can be an expert in your own. So make sure you're balancing your thinking about what you can do differently to remove barriers for Black colleagues with an examination of how is it that you don't have those same barriers: How is it I don't have to worry about being late? How is it I can get sponsored or can find mentors really easily? How can I simply step into any space, and not have anybody question my presence? Or even how is it that my corporate culture, this organization that I run, works so well for people who look like me? How is it that, no matter how much we've committed to diversity and inclusion, we continue to perpetuate these outcomes that are so favourable to the majority of our white workforce, but so unfavourable for Black colleagues?

These are the questions, based on your experience, that will elicit far more insight when they are combined with insights from your Black colleagues, than those from purely focusing on the Black experience alone, because the unintended consequences of overly focusing on trying to be an expert here is that you imply that Black colleagues are broken and they need fixing. Also, in focusing on becoming an expert, you are considering Black people as a collective rather than as individuals.

> *How about we stop viewing people as the colour of the skin and start looking at the content of their character, since we all bleed red. Every single one of us. Let's fix it and move on to ask more important questions like: why are people trying to divide us?*
>
> Data engineer, 2021

In this fashion, in your reach of expertise, it's almost like you're looking to see if there is something in the way Black people think, or the way Black people do things, that is actually contributing to the problem. Rather than acknowledging or understanding that structural racism is the problem, in your 'expertise' you are perpetuating systemic racism by considering a fault within Black people, their work ethic and ability to 'fit' into societal norms. Do you recognise the issues with solely turning your lens externally, when you need to look internally?

One of the best pieces of advice for executive leadership teams as a whole is to become experts on your experience, and ask yourself questions surrounding some of the turning points that form the decisions that you make, and the support that you've gotten, individually and as a team, along the way for you to get to your position of power and rank. What can you learn from this new knowledge? It's akin to deconstructing your career history. So straightaway you're starting to think, hang on a minute, that's a really good point. How did I get here? What were some of those defining life moments where I had support or, potentially, where things weren't as difficult for me as they might be for others? Now that you have considered your lived experience, it is possible in comparison to consider what you understand about other people's lived experiences.

When everyone on the executive team is thinking about their own experiences, you can begin to challenge each other. As a corporate leader, think about when you hired your chief financial officer or chief marketing officer, for example, particularly if they all look like you. And have the discussion that questions how easy it is to fill a room with people who look like us, but examines how it is that we don't have any Black people at executive level, or actually don't have any representation below executive level. So why does 'what works really well for us' not work well for Black colleagues? That's the dynamic that unfortunately is missing.

This work is about gaining insights into personal experience. It is not a platform for white fragility and self-sensitivity surrounding how you, your board and your organization treat Black colleagues. You are putting your experiences under a microscope and challenging each other about how those experiences came about. You ask the questions and at the back of your mind always keep thinking about your current workplace culture and what that culture represents, and forever ask yourself why your culture works so well for people who look like you.

And consider what can you learn from this.

> *Racism is an ideology. Let's talk about how it manifests itself in the workplace. Let's talk about what it means to live in a racialised society versus a post-racialised society.*
>
> Shereen Daniels, 2021

What about Colleagues Resistant to Change?

It's all well and good when your executive teams are all on board, however, how do you reconcile with colleagues who are a little bit slow in getting with the programme (for want of a better phrase), or who are either passively or even actively resisting some of the introspective work, soon to become initiatives, that you're trying to level with your colleagues?

Here we are talking about people who may feel resentful about the space you are giving to the issue of racism, who feel like they are being made to feel guilty for being white, as if this is an attack on them (and it's not their fault that racism is a thing), or the intensity of what you're doing is too much and you're not doing a lot more for everyone in the company because all lives matter.

These are the colleagues for whom your introspective approach has made them question whether there's a place for them in your organization because you've changed the microscope. Until this point, they've been able to bask in the glory of the way that things have always been done, the systems and process that have unfairly benefited them over everyone else and all of a sudden, in their mind, you're taking some of that sunlight and redistributing it to Black colleagues, and considering doing things that will actually never benefit them.

There is no easy way to answer this, but let's shed a little perspective on the situation. First, this has come up in pretty much every single organization I have ever worked with concerning their advancement towards racial equity. And believe me, I've spoken to many.

> *My company introduced reverse mentoring. Initially I was excited at the thought of having more face time with a board director. But after a few sessions, I realised he was using them to educate himself about racism. How is that supposed to help me? And I can't say anything because of who he is. I wish I had never said yes.*
>
> Data analyst, 2020

Think about the saying 'energy flows where attention goes'. If you are resolute in dismantling systemic racism in your organization, because you've doing the introspective work and are making informed and conscious decisions about the steps you're now ready to take to become an anti-racist company, and are considering ways to ensure that your culture is inclusive, focus your energy there. Carry on with the initiative, and don't second guess or doubt what you're trying to achieve. Because if you're worried about how it's going to be perceived by your colleagues who are anti-equity or against the 'sudden' focus on Black colleagues, the colleagues who may not be anti-equality but don't want to do anything differently to get there, you will spend a disproportionate amount of time and energy placating those colleagues. All the while missing a massive opportunity to empower, enable and mobilise the colleagues who fully support your plan. Your energy will be focused in the wrong direction.

You have colleagues who want to be part of the solution and are ready to be active allies, colleagues who are ready to speak truth to power, and are committed to leveraging and sharing their power and influence. They know they can get away with saying certain things because their identity, position and privilege affords them a level of protection their Black colleagues just don't have. Yet even they are being sidelined because you're so conscious about a small group of naysayers who don't want to get with the programme and may never get there.

Shift your focus and always keep thinking about the overarching vision of the organization that you want to build and the culture that you're trying to evolve. Focus on what you stand to gain, not what you might lose. You're not going to get there overnight; it is going to take a lot of work over many years. But you know this – through the work you're doing, you're choosing to future-proof your organization, and mitigate corporate risk ten or twenty years down the line. You already know that dismantling racism within your organization isn't a single-year financial commitment. (At least, by now, I hope you know this.)

Therefore you want to put your energy there. Make advancing racial equity so irresistible and so sticky that you are already starting to be a magnet for colleagues, suppliers and customers (if you choose to share what you're doing). All the while you're taking steps, across the fence other leaders are still debating whether they even want to have the conversation, never mind doing anything about it.

Align with other organizations who share your anti-racist values. This is important for you in terms of support but it also shows your Black colleagues that the issues of systemic racism are important enough for you to put specific time and energy into addressing it. What you're saying is that, as a business, you are disrupting white supremacy, that you will no longer find it acceptable to be an organization that only shows up for the homogenous 'majority', and that your organization will now begin to factor in how lived experiences and different barriers affect Black people. And you're okay with prioritising where you see fit, because when you put all of that together what you're saying is: We pride ourselves in being a business that values difference in every context.

If you focus on the forward trajectory of where you're trying to go – innovating, experimenting, finding ways to empower your colleagues to advance racial equity, giving them knowledge and the tools to be able to move from introspection to action – then this becomes your new normal.

This evolves into the definition of your standard business practice, and it thus becomes harder for any colleagues who are resistant to change to want to remain part of your company. Making anti-racism and racial equity the culture of the majority will make it harder for those who still harbour resentment and anger to stick around. The saboteurs – whether silent or vocal – must make a decision about whether your organization is the right place for them to be, or whether they should leave. You have to make a decision about whether you are okay with losing those colleagues. In my line of work, this is not always a given.

Rather than spending so much time talking and debating and worrying about this reluctant group, focus on empowering colleagues, keeping your feedback loops going and ensuring you continue to reiterate why dismantling racism is important to you. Keep telling the narrative, keep sharing, keep allowing people in and bring them closer, amplifying different voices and different experiences, even to the extent of bringing outsiders in if you have to, because at this point you need to become the workplace culture you say you want. And you can't do that if you're always spending your time and energy focused on the few people (no matter how senior they are) who don't get it.

If you are struggling to readjust your lens to focus on the colleagues who do get it and do want to be part of the solution, sit with that for a moment. Is it because you are projecting your fears, your discomfort? Or is it because you're worried that you have an underlying current of racism within a larger population of your workforce than you first thought, and to do deal with that means you'll have to take some sort of action?

I'm deliberately not offering you any assurances or reassurance here. This is something you will have to work through; we have already covered the why of these uncomfortable feelings earlier in the book.

The brave and bold leaders are the ones who make their stance very clear. They are the ones who say that if you want to be part of this culture, this organization that I'm building, that we're building, then advancing racial equity must be part of your workplace parameters. If you don't agree, then you're more than welcome to leave.

This may seem harsh, and yet the reverse of this happens regularly. There are organizations whose founders don't want to engage in issues of social justice, and don't want to think about how they can be part of the solution, so much so that they want to completely divorce their company from reality. They've got no shame in doing do, saying, in effect, you can come to work for us provided that you don't talk about how your lived experiences impact on your experience in our workplace; that you don't talk about some of society's most challenging issues and how we can come together to be part of the solution; and that you only talk about things directly connected to the products or services that we sell. You can only engage in things where we think there is a direct financial payoff, or that we feel is easy or comfortable for us to engage with, or that affects 'all of us', not just the few.

Those businesses are out there, and we hear more and more about the stance that they're taking. Twitter is a gold mine if you want to do some digging on your own.

This is all part of the foundational introspection, recognising where the problems are and making a conscious decision about what you do next. From this point on across each of the following Four-Factor RACE Model steps, not only are you aiming to become anti-racist, but you are actively looking for ways to remove racism and structural barriers within your organization. You will also be actively advancing racial equity, considering ways in which to level the playing field. Not to help Black colleagues – remember, they're not broken – but in recognition that your workplace culture currently serves a certain part of your workforce.

You need to say to yourself regularly that this journey is going to be challenging. That you recognise that not everybody is going to be onboard with where your new vision is taking the organization, but you are ready to start leading the change. And all you can do is hope you make it as sexy as hell for the detractors, for them to have no choice but to be curious that you're going to keep finding ways to make it irresistible, and for them not to stray from your new corporate direction. And you're not going to spend your time pandering to those who want to put a spanner in the works, just because they feel uncomfortable or even – unpalatable yet true – harbour racist views, because you know, and like I said at the beginning, energy flows where attention goes.

Across 2020 we were repeatedly shown that the world isn't what we thought. We can no longer pretend that what happens in other nations has nothing to do with us. In the same way, we cannot pretend that what happens within our communities, postcodes, workplaces and country has nothing to do with us.

I liken it to all of us sitting in our conservatories, our havens away from work, looking through the glass at our gardens beyond. Over the years, we became so used to seeing the same view day in and day out that we never noticed the accumulation of dirt on the windows. Then someone came along and cleaned the windows, and we realised our garden isn't in the shape we thought it was. Ignoring it and carrying on regardless is an option (otherwise known as feigning ignorance). Or you can put on your gardening gloves and get to work. The weeds cannot uproot themselves.

Shereen Daniels, 2021

Analyse the Impact

Compelled by your ongoing introspective work, there will come a point where you'll want to access your organization's data in order to analyse the impact that systemic racism has on your workforce. Hopefully your curiosity will drive you towards this second factor and you'll realise that advancing racial equity is akin to building a plane whilst flying at the same time. You'll find the Four Factors that make up the RACE Model are not sequential. Recognising the problems you face is an ongoing process that continues when you pick up the mantle of the next stage: Analyse the Impact.

When it comes to analysing the current impact systemic racism has in their organizations, everyone assumes the answer starts and stops with racism. And it could be. The data you already collect may show an ethnicity pay gap, inequitable promotion rates and asymmetric attrition rates. But racism is too simple an answer. If that's your only answer, where do you go from there? How do you know what interventions to put in place? How do you measure impact?

You need to use a system that brings your organization into its own space of where it is starting from, not where companies and society in general stand. Systemic racism is going to manifest itself in different ways for every person and organization, because everyone has slightly different ways of doing things, of creating systems. So for single trends the work has to be specific.

In essence, Analyse the Impact is about organizational analysis using both qualitative and quantitative data.

Quantitative data is just one of two pieces of the data puzzle. It's the default one that everyone loves because it's factual, logical and can be used to validate or invalidate ideas, experiences or courses of action. It also fits nicely in spreadsheets, and in theory it allows logical conclusions to be drawn. Qualitative data includes stories. Words. Experiences of your colleagues, partners, suppliers and your communities at large.

Don't dismiss qualitative data of your Black colleagues' lived experiences, including Black candidates who applied for positions. You can contact people who have already left and ask if they are willing to have a conversation about their experiences. Don't rely only on the data you can quantify in spreadsheets and reports, because stories and experiences will bring that data to life.

This is the data between data and insights. Data is raw, unprocessed facts gathered within a particular timeframe using a particular method of collection. Insights, however, give you context. They tell a story and allow you to examine correlations and patterns.

The combination of these two types of data will give you an outline of the specific challenges you face. This precise approach will be more helpful than digesting streams of external reports only to conclude, 'Well that's great, but how do I apply that to us?'

Centring the Voices of Colleagues Most Impacted

For a very long time your Black colleagues have felt silenced and ignored. Or maybe they didn't and have always felt like your culture was one in which they could be their authentic selves, knowing that when issues arose of racism and discrimination, the values you espouse would spring to life and they would be consistently treated with dignity and respect.

Do you know how your Black colleagues feel? Not just after an overt racist incident has played out the media and you've reached out to ask if they are okay. How does it feel for them every day? What would they like to see you do differently? What would they say if there was no fear or concerns about retaliation?

Part of Analysing the Impact is opening the door for colleagues to share their experiences about what it's like to be Black within your organization. Typically, many companies engaged in this activity soon after the murder of George Floyd, but some never created that space. Or if they did, it was a one-off and the business carried on regardless.

You centre the voices of those impacted by racism and discrimination by listening. Frequently. Over and over again.

Part of the reason why I have been able to amass so many conversations about this is because I and my colleagues are often asked to run listening forums for organizations. Initially it was at the height of Black Lives Matter, but as time went on, companies also began using them to enable feedback.

In other words, a listening forum is a communication and engagement tool to help you centre the voices of your Black colleagues so they feel seen and heard.

You would usually run these with an external facilitator who is skilled in quickly creating a psychologically safe environment for your employees to share their experiences and how they feel about particular issues that obstruct them from feeling like they belong within your culture.

Listening forums put your colleagues at the centre, so they can speak freely, using their words, sharing their stories without being interrupted by well-meaning managers or directors who listen with an intent to respond, not with an intent to hear. This raises awareness and sets an organization-wide context for why this is important. When you as the CEO open a forum like this and talk about your reflections, from an honest and vulnerable place, it allows your colleagues to see how genuine you are in addressing the impact of racism for the betterment of all your teams, but particularly your Black colleagues.

If you do decide to run your own version of a listening forum, bear the following in mind:

Lead from the front. The most senior person in your organization (CEO/founder) must lead the communications in the run-up to the forum, open the forum, and send the follow-up communications after the event.

If your workforce senses that there is not a genuine desire to make meaningful change, you will lose any opportunity to build trust and show commitment. Devolving this responsibility to your chief people officer or diversity, equity and inclusion lead is frankly a cop-out.

Devolve the choice of facilitator. Give your teams a sense of the person you are bringing in to facilitate the forum. If possible, show-case examples of their work (e.g. articles they have written, interviews they have done in this area, testimonials, or clips of videos/social media interactions), which can help allay fears and concerns.

It is important your colleagues feel that the person you bring in is credible, understands their perspective and isn't someone who is too 'corporate' or lacks authenticity.

This is where a listening forum differs from a traditional keynote event. The emphasis here is on psychological safety and support.

Ask, don't dictate. When you publicise the forum, ask for volunteers who feel comfortable sharing their perspectives or stories about racism, or how they feel as a Black person within your business. Even though you may already know who is vocal, this must be a choice that people can freely exercise rather than feeling there is an expectation for them to say yes if you approach them directly.

It is not about scripted experiences, but you need to ask for an idea of what your employees want to talk about so you can make sure you have fresh angles to explore and discuss during the forum.

In addition, it's imperative your HR team follows up with every single person who expressed an interest yet wasn't chosen. These employees have clearly signalled they want to talk, so reach out to them to be certain they feel heard and supported.

Make sure there is a debriefing session afterwards. A few days after the forum, when the dust has settled, regroup with the facilitator to discuss feedback, observations and how both your Black and non-Black colleagues responded/reacted to the forum. Ensure there is adequate support for Black colleagues who may have been triggered by what they heard.

Listening forums are one of the most transformational exercises you can do, but you have to handle them with sensitivity and care. Your colleagues shouldn't have to wait for permission for the business to listen. What they share in this context is valuable to you – only if you do something about it.

How have you elicited the feedback of your Black colleagues so far? Is it time to go back and talk to them again?

Gathering Your Data

Whether it's because of the introspective journey you've been on in Recognise the Problem, or your processing of some of the lived experiences your colleagues shared during your version of a listening forum, you are likely to have many unanswered questions swirling around in your mind.

Why did I not know any of this? Why is my organization so white? How come I didn't pay too much attention before? Why in all my meetings does everyone look like me? Why are there no Black people in our leadership pipeline? Why do we have hardly any in senior leadership positions?

Wait a minute. . .where are all the Black people?

And why?

It's important to realise that you and your organization are a single trend and your answers, and the journey you take to reach those answers, are specific to you. As a result, you won't find an exhaustive list of data that you can tick boxes against especially when you're starting out. The best advice this book can give is to use any data from any reporting system, spreadsheet or database you can get your hands on, as many data points as you muster, including any customer or end user data you have, that can be tied back to ethnicity.

If your organization has never collated ethnicity data, you may decide to ask your workplace for this information. This approach depends on the level of trust your workforce has with your organization, and any request requires honesty and integrity. Start with 'I. . .', and not 'We, as an organization. . .' So when colleagues consider entering their data, they are doing so because your personal values align, and their input is based on their trust and belief in your values as a leader. It might be that you just have to put a line in the sand and from a certain date forward ask new colleagues to include their ethnicity data, rather than request it from your current workforce. However, the opportunity to collate ethnicity data for your colleagues and communicate your anti-racist journey as it unfolds is one not to miss, so suck it up and be honest with your teams, and ask them if they wouldn't mind parting with the information.

Of course, you can't make it compulsory, but any data you can get will pay off in the future. If you have ethnicity data already, then the next stage is simply approaching the right people to access it, such as looking at ethnicity in relation to your payroll data. You literally go to your payroll person and ask them to export an anonymised version of ethnicity against their pay grade and bonus structure. And then your curiosity will take over: what's the difference in pay between Black people and white people? What's the difference with gender? And if you are in the situation where you've requested this data from your workforce because it has not been collated previously, collect as much information as possible, for example, concerning gender, disability, sexual identification. Think about other identities you might want to know about and ask for it all in one fell swoop, all the while remembering to choose your terminology intentionally and with care.

Collecting information across the spectrum of individuality enables you to demonstrate how addressing racial equity has a positive impact on other marginalised groups, which in turn fits into your wider corporate inclusion plan and the overall transformative change taking place in the organization's DNA. It makes you more conscious of intersectionality, ensuring that rather than starting at ground zero for other marginalised communities, you're layering on top with more nuance and more context, according to your other colleagues' lived experience.

All of this gathered information will start to paint a picture about how inequalities are manifesting itself within your organization. You are likely to be a whirlwind of questions: What about promotions? Who's been promoted at what frequency? How many Black people do we have in our leadership teams? On the next level and the next level, and the one after that? Where does the concrete ceiling hit for a Black colleague versus a white colleague? Who's leaving? Who's joining? Who gets the opportunity to take on glamour projects? To be sponsored and enabled to spend time shadowing very senior people in your organization?

These are all important questions that your data points will feed into, and within it all it's worth keeping in mind the one question that is never asked enough: Why does my organizational culture work for people who look like me?

For white people.

Oh yes, we analysed our data and we definitely have issues with racism, so now we've got a consultant who is updating our policies, and we've just had budget sign-off to implement a new applicant tracking system to reduce bias.

HR business partner, 2021

A Brief Note about Classification

For UK organizations, to make life easier for you, it is recommended you use the Office for National Statistics (ONS) classifications to collect ethnicity data. It's not perfect, but it does allow you to provide a credible methodology that is already in place when ethnicity pay gap reporting becomes mandatory and/or when you need to disclose your metrics to shareholders and key stakeholders.

Visit the Office for National Statistics (https://www.ons.gov.uk/) for the most up-to-date classifications.

Representation

Before commencing your analysis, bring together a group of colleagues to work on the gathered data with you. The task at hand requires group thinking (different from group think), yet with the colleagues you bring together and your organization as a whole, it's important to recognise that there is no correlation between representation and the presence of racism, or lack thereof.

You can have the most ethnically representative business in the world, but it doesn't mean you don't have an issue with racism.

I will say this one more time. You can have the most ethnically representative business in the world, but it doesn't mean you don't have an issue with racism.

As considered in Chapter 1, representation is about output – a very visual output. It is easily constructed through a tokenistic approach to systemic racism that, rather than analyse the inputs that founded your organization's racist processes and systems, applies a veneer of transformative change. But it is fear driven, built on nothing more than a need to mitigate corporate risk. And it doesn't work, because the systems underneath representational output remain as racist as they were before you put a few Black faces on the cover of your corporate brochure.

Transformative change goes beyond what's represented in communities. If you are advancing racial equity in your organization and your systems and processes are anti-racist, your talented workforce might, at any one point, consist of 90% Black people or 90% white people. And if that's the case, it's not because of structural racism.

The issue we have within our society is that there are so many layers of racism structured into our way of life we've never dealt with that we still think visual representation is a sign of progress, but it's nothing more than an output. When you understand, for example, what's prohibiting Black people from progressing in your organization or getting through your recruitment process, and the key word here is 'prohibiting', you begin to recognise the structural barriers in place that favour white people. It's systemic because it is a pattern that is replicated in organizations all over the world, in territories with a history of chattel slavery, colonialism and/or imperialism. Analysing the impact of racism moves your thinking from tokenism and representation to authentic transformative change, where increased representation becomes one of the outputs, not the only one.

Further, remember data is also an output. It measures things after the fact. It measures the what, not the why. So never treat it as an input; hold in your mind that the data is telling you the story after the horse has bolted. It doesn't tell you the story of how the horse got to the stable in the first place or why the door was unlocked.

(Dis)engagement Surveys

It's funny because we've been running engagement surveys for years and we've never seen an issue with racism. It's come out of the blue.

Chief people officer, 2020

Too often executive leaders are quick to task their HR lead with restructuring the results of their latest engagement survey to disprove the notion that there is an issue with systemic racism in their business.

Engagement surveys have become an industry where organizations can lie. There are countless examples of companies wanting to create their own questions to elicit a specific answer and/or a response that skims over any real issues and instead reinforces what executive leaders would like to hear.

Remember, engagement surveys are supposed to provide a feedback loop to allow colleagues to share how they feel about their role, their line manager, your leadership and the culture of your organization – to varying degrees, of course. The problem is that they rarely give an accurate reflection of what's going on in the workplace.

Think about the last engagement (or similar) survey you ran:

- How often do your colleagues have an opportunity to formally give feedback on how they are feeling and being managed? Once a year? Twice a year?

- Did your survey allow your colleagues to share their experiences, directly or indirectly, of racism and discrimination?
- Can your Black colleagues anonymously share their feelings and perspectives about how you as a company have addressed anti-racism to date?
- Did your survey ask enough questions for you to understand how ethnicity intersects with other identities (for example, in the areas of religion or gender) and therefore what the colleague experience looks like?
- Do you ask about how safe your colleagues feel in being able to speak up about their experiences and know that their manager will listen and act?
- What were the response rates split by ethnicity? By gender? By religion?
- What is the cost of disengagement to your organization? Is that a price you are prepared to pay?

A lot of us have been taught and raised that we shouldn't be too emotional. From a neuroscience perspective, that's impossible. And what we have seen in our data is that if you don't allow people to be emotional at work, it reduces their productivity and it reduces their creativity. So the question is, do people who are minoritised feel safe to share their emotions at work? If not, why not? And what are CEOs prepared to do about that?

Matt Phelan, co-founder, Happiness Index

Turning Data into Insights

Decision makers will very quickly cite that a lack of representation is the problem, typically believing that is where they should start.

HR might offer up that they are still trying to collate ethnicity data for their colleagues to enable better evaluation, but beyond the usual attraction, retention and development metrics, what else could you or should you be looking at?

Following are some examples.

Attraction and Retention

1. How is your employer brand perceived by Black candidates?
2. Would they come and work for you? If not, why not? What would you need to demonstrate for your organization to be an attractive destination for them?
3. What are the attrition rates for your Black colleagues? What are the exit interviews telling you?
4. How do you rate on external employer review sites? Are there consistent themes appearing?
5. What percentage of Black colleagues have formal sponsors?

Succession Planning

6. Where are your Black colleagues within your succession plans?
7. How many different roles, on average, do they perform during their tenure? How does this compare to non-Black colleagues?
8. Which colleagues were given promotions with just a 'tap on the shoulder' versus who had to apply?

Learning and Development

9. Who has been on formal learning and development programs? Had external courses paid for?
10. Conversely, if you are looking to put in place a Black leadership development programme, for example, are you say-

ing that the white colleagues who have been promoted all went on a version of a programme too? Is there a consistency in approach? How can you demonstrate that?

Pay and Reward

11. What is your ethnicity pay gap?

12. Who has long-term incentive plans and share options as an exception to their job grade, for example?

13. Who has been given additional benefits, outside of 'job needs'?

14. What about bonus payout? Not so much the amount, but when you make discretionary arrangements, when colleagues or the business has not hit the bonus trigger, who gets what, how much and why?

15. How do you award pay increases? Who gets the standard and who gets the above 'inflation'? How are you challenging the decision-making of the line manager or director?

16. Who is getting a pay increase outside of your annual cycle? Who is authorising that? Why? How are they able to circumvent the standard process?

17. Who is denied a pay rise? Who is the person doing the declining? Why? And what other pay decisions has this line manager or director made?

18. If you took all your available pay and reward data, added in grade, gender and other characteristics or identities, what else does it tell you?

19. Which colleagues benefit the most from your informal recognition programmes? How does that compare to your formal initiatives? For example, are your Black colleagues getting the majority of the informal praise, but consistently overlooked for promotions or repeatedly having pay reviews declined?

20. How far are all of these questions asked and discussed during your remuneration committee (or equivalent) meetings? If not, why not?

Performance Management

21. What is the correlation between someone's performance grade and their pay and remuneration?
22. What is the correlation to grade and promotions, based on what actually happens, not hypothetically?
23. Who is captured as top talent? Who is ready for stretch assignments?
24. How do you stress-test that your performance management evaluation processes are robust and bias free?

Employee Relations

25. How many cases of racism and racial discrimination have been reported? What was the outcome? How many formal sanctions were issued? What happened to the colleagues who raised the issues? Are they still in the business?
26. How many settlement agreements have been created? For whom? How much? And why?
27. If you have a zero-tolerance approach to racism, how do you enforce that? Is it without exception?

Supply Chain

28. How many suppliers are Black owned or Black led?
29. What proportion of your spend is going to white-owned/led businesses? Why is that?
30. What are your payment terms?
31. What is the process involved for onboarding new suppliers? How far does it support your assertions of equitable treatment for all?

Customers/Clients

32. What are your customers and clients saying online?

33. How do they feel about a corporation's responsibility to be part of the solution?

34. Are your clients taking action? Your competitors? What are they doing and saying? Does it matter?

Root Cause Analysis

At this point you've gathered all of the generic data points possible, plus any that may be specific to your organization. Next you want to engage in root cause analysis (RCA) because it is not enough to take a spreadsheet, input a clever formula that considers the data against ethnicity and outputs racism as the cause of inequity. A conclusion of racism helps no one. You need to determine the underlying reasons why.

The best way to do this is to take each data point, and ask yourself a question: Why is this happening?

When you answer that question, don't stop there. Ask it again, why is this happening?

Why is this happening?

Why is this happening?

Why is this happening?

It takes at least five why's.

The intent here is to turn data – a raw collection of facts – into insights by applying the 'why'.

This is a perfect principle because when you go underneath the superficial to get to the bottom of 'why', you can have a look at some of the founding reasons behind the existence of certain things in your organization, allowing you to determine where you want to focus your organization's time, energy and effort. This is not possible with an answer of racism on its own. And because RCA is based on data rather than emotion, because the process is about solving problems, no one is singled out or blamed for the results. The team is working to co-create solutions. And yes, you can still do this exercise even if you don't have the lived experience, because you can use your own experience as an opportunity to get insights. Remember, the objective is not to become an expert in the Black experience.

So RCA can be done digitally, or even old school with a white board and a pack of Post-it notes. And this is how you get started.

Across the top of your RCA, post all your data points within their specific categories. This way it is easy to assess what the data is telling you, whether that is an ethnicity pay gap, a higher turnover for Black colleagues and so on. Once you've outlined this exercise, it's a good idea to bring in the team of people mentioned previously who are interested in taking part as the process gets quite involved. If you already have an anti-racism task force then this is their jam, but if you don't, communicate across departments for interested parties who want to be part of the anti-racist solution to come and help.

When you've got your team together and you've outlined your data points and categories, take a step back. Recognise you can't solve everything within your organization, and that the amalgam of data presented on your white board may feel overwhelming for the whole team. This is the time to have the conversation about what you want to sort out and why. Why are these the areas you wish to prioritise? And don't waiver from them. This is time to focus on the specifics.

Within each issue the data presents, when you get to the last of your five (or six, seven or eight) why's, the answer, invariably in some cases, delivers racism. Remember, racism isn't just about individual acts of behaviour; it is also about the combination of systems, policies and behaviours woven together that have never been questioned based on what's happened within your organization historically, where outcomes always favour white people. This is why pay is an issue, and promotions too. You need to go deeper and delve into the processes and procedures that frame your workplace. Therefore it's important to reiterate that every organization is going to have a slightly different way in which racism manifests itself. So don't just jump to the first why and make assumptions (i.e. this data plus this data means racism), because you will miss some valuable insights that will unravel through continuous questioning and data interrogation.

The Foundations of a Good Problem Statement

Before your team gets into the 'why', it's important to make each problem statement you're assessing precise and clear for everyone involved, so set the following two ground rules:

Rule One: Empower one person to facilitate the whole process.

This individual will be the one asking the 'why' questions. To be honest, it's a fun role, but you can't ask the question and be part of the team looking for answers, so perhaps get someone external to the team to be your interrogative 'why' person.

Rule Two: Answers should be based on real data rather than emotional opinions.

This prevents moments of frustration from creeping in when you just want to shout, 'It's racism!' And yes, the chances are the data is demonstrating an example of racism. There's no question that, for example, pay inequity between white and Black colleagues is racist, but it is telling you this after the fact that it has happened. Remember, data is an outcome. It is a tool for you to interrogate and discover why it exists, as it does in the first place. It is racism. But why is it racism?

Further, in the first five minutes of your meeting, make sure that everyone is clear on the problem at hand as generated by the data. Ensure you have each team member's specific agreement that when the problem is written down or spoken about, they know and agree what the problem is. This sounds very basic. But if no one agrees on the problem, no one's ever going to agree on a solution, because they're all thinking about a different problem.

Always just take a moment and say, right, what's the problem statement here?

RCA Example

Where RCA is really useful is in its ability to connect action to the root cause of a problem, something that often gets missed when tackling large issues such as systemic racism. These can get abstract really quickly if solutions are not tied directly to the issues set out in your organization's data. Following is a case in point.

> *Consider:* Within your internal communications request for ethnicity data from your staff, you also asked bellwether questions concerning the respondents' views on the executive board's commitment to dismantling racism within your organization.
>
> *Problem:* Over half of the respondents do not feel executive leadership is committed to anti-racism.
>
> *Why do over half of the respondents feel this way:* No one believes the executive board is serious about anti-racism because there has been a lack of action to date, and targets are basic.
>
> *Why have the targets been basic:* Because it's an organizational culture to do the minimum standard, rather than go above and beyond.

Why is this the organizational culture: Because it's based on showing activity rather than progress.

Why is showing progress inhibited: The organization has a really low risk appetite.

Why do they have a low risk appetite: They are concerned with what could go wrong if they get this wrong. They are concerned with reputational risk and don't want to be accused of doing anything that could cause reputational risk. The low risk appetite is driven by fear.

The perception is that they're not doing enough because they're playing it safe, and therefore they are not trusted by colleagues. Fear underlies executive leadership inertia.

Equity Actions and Equity Goals

So this example of trust and fear demonstrates a depth of analysis most organizations don't get into. We're used to taking information from spreadsheets and databases and actioning them before Excel (or Google Sheets) even has a chance to load.

With this in mind, when you've got to the root cause of the data, which in this case is fear, what you can do collectively – as a team, not you on your own – is lessen that root cause, the fear. Because if you can lessen the fear, then you can put actions in place that have more impact: equity actions based on equity goals. And if you can put these impactful actions in place in a way that isn't going to damage the reputation of the organization, you're fundamentally going to be able to make a difference for your Black colleagues. If you can make a difference for your Black colleagues, they are going to feel like the executive board have taken dismantling racism seriously. If your Black colleagues feel like the board are taking it seriously, they then trust when the board says, 'We are committed to anti-racism'. They believe them.

Imagine you did this for your entire executive team. You went through this exercise with them. At first, at 'why' number one and two, everyone on the team will have plenty to say, but by the time you've got to your fifth or even eighth 'why', the room goes quiet. Because you're getting into the very fabric of the issues and no one has truly thought them through. And the point that you're making with your now very quiet executive team is that if one person as an individual is feeling this fear and you multiply that fear by eight people, or the fourteen members of your executive team sitting in front of you around the table, is it any wonder that we are never going to be able to make the progress needed, because fundamentally we are driven by compounded fear?

Facilitating an RCA session gives you a different, more impactful output than just having a generalised discussion about data patterns. Rather than just being enabled to say no to anti-racist initiatives without any in-depth understanding of why, you've increased the awareness of their own fear that is holding back the organization, and possibly confronted your own at the same time.

This is what makes RCA so powerful, because it turns on light bulbs in people's minds that they wouldn't ordinarily think about. If a colleague had said to you, 'I don't trust the executive team', and off the bat you asked them, 'Why do you think that?' you would have never gotten to this point about fear, the innate fear that's wrapped around the organization holding you back from advancing racial equity and maintaining the privileged status quo for white colleagues.

Creating the space to explore the RCA of inequities means you end up with a list of succinct, defined issues with context. You now understand the 'what' and can move on to explaining the 'why'.

And any progress you make will aggregate, like compound interest. Transformative small changes mobilise further change.

Why Does Our Organization Work So Well for White People?

Okay, so RCA exercises work in lots of different ways. You can do the five 'why's' with your executive board, with your peers. You can do them with other colleagues and say, 'Why do you think this is?' And when you say that, it stops people feeling like they need to be experts in the Black experience and it forces them to think about their experience, taking the onus of dismantling racism away from an existence as a project to support helpless Black colleagues. It stops white people from white saviourism and from asking, 'Why can't Black colleagues succeed here?' as though there is something wrong with them. Instead, it makes them focus on the system that benefits white people. RCA enables anyone who isn't Black to be experts on their own experience, but you need to help people think about it.

> *I feel like our company is always asking us for the answers, but why don't they ask the white managers why they aren't promoting us? Why do they only hire one or two Black people in their team?*
> Sales associate, 2021

But once they start answering the question, honestly, you might have ten levels of why, and they're still going as you're unraveling a really powerful question, all the while looking at it from your own experience, rather than 'othering' and second-guessing a Black colleague's experience.

When you do this you're tapping into how people consider what their life was like in their runup to joining your organization, what life was like as they have climbed the ranks, or did things differently, or just existed. And then they realise that they can only ever be experts in their own experience. But we are very rarely asked questions that tap into that. So there's always a feeling like we have to be an expert on somebody else to come up with the solutions.

And the answers you come up with can give you the equity actions for what can be done within the organization's systems and processes to support Black colleagues' advancement. This is really helpful in putting systems in place when your organization doesn't have Black colleagues. You might not have Black colleagues because your recruitment company doesn't put CVs from Black people in front of you, because you never employ Black people. They might have a perception based on the lack of representation in your business that you actually don't want Black people in the door. Or they've sent Black people to you before and you've not taken them. Or they've already got one other Black candidate on the shortlist.

The work can already commence, so when your new anti-racist hiring process gets underway, your workplace is already more inclusive for your new Black colleagues. You don't need to find a Black person and put them under the microscope and ask them 50,000 questions about 'solving racism' in your workplace. You can break all of this down from your experience and that of your white colleagues.

Progressive Inclusion

People will buy into something if they feel like they've got choice, which is a pain in the bloody neck.

But when you arrive at this, understanding the reasoning that follows enables you to leverage their inclusion. So rather than going at 100 miles an hour to your version of utopia based on your frustrations, and your lived experiences of the world, and what you think needs to change, you go back a step and ask what others need to change.

Now, how can you value everybody's lived experience when the purpose of racial equity is that you're putting things in place to address the structural issues and barriers that affect Black colleagues? This doesn't mean you're ignoring everybody else. You just have to put in a different set of actions. And so you're not saying that a Black person's lived experience is more important in this context. But what you are saying is that the society in which we live, and unfortunately, how things manifest in your organization, places more value on white lived experience than on Black lived experience. You are not comparing traumas, but what you are saying is that we have made a choice to prioritise this for the benefit of everyone.

You can't fix everything, but you have the opportunity to make more change within the four walls of your organization than society at large. You are not constrained by institutions, economic structures and a criminal justice system built upon unfair laws and enshrined in the very foundations in which we live, work and play.

Change is yours for the making.

Expectations and Reality

Racial equity work is culture change. Dismantling systemic racism is culture change. When you start to break it down, some of the work you do will directly impact the way your organization operates. This could be another problem, but one that's got nothing to do with dismantling racism and racial equity, although these will still be a challenge.

> *You're told: 'If you work hard enough and you do the right things, you can move up in this company,' he said. That's no longer the case.. . .They're only promoting Black people. This is reverse discrimination against white people.*
> Anonymous employee, cited in Koenig, 2021

Some colleagues will believe the organization is moving too fast and changing too quickly, and some will consider the changes are being made at a glacial pace. You need to think about ways in which you can connect the dots to help your colleagues realise what is happening, and why change is happening at the pace it is. First, you shouldn't be doing this on your own. If you left on a sabbatical, for example, the organization's wheels of advancing racial equity should still be turning. You are a person to enable the organization to explore the issues at hand rather than personally fix them. Because if you get into a 'fix them' mentality, you're also part of the problem.

And it becomes about your pace rather than the organization's. At the level of communication required through RCA, you need other people on board. This is why change is so difficult if your executive team don't buy in to your anti-racist values, why the people executing change can be singled out if they don't have support from their line management, and why as CEO you need to make your new values as sexy as hell to get others on side.

Single Point of Failure

Throughout the process you need to make sure that it is not one person's plan – not your plan, or your HR lead's plan or anyone else. You do not need to give people a reason to say, 'Well they just came up with that'. If it works well, then it's great being the single point of success, but if it doesn't and needs to be tweaked or reanalysed due to continuity changes, for example, then you become the single point of failure, which leaves you thinking, 'Well, hang on a minute. I thought we all agreed?'

The biggest mistake that organizations make in trying to address systemic racism is that they make one person or even two or three people the points of failure because they expect those individuals to come up with and implement all the solutions. The power should lie with the extended groups that you are a part of, co-creating solutions alongside those people who are most impacted by systemic racism. Thus, in the event of any setbacks, they should not become finger-pointing exercises. The responsibility doesn't lie solely on one person's shoulders.

> *We have dozens of members, some of whom have served on corporate boards and recognise that the chances of them continuing to serve on boards because they are white and male have been greatly diminished by this new quota rule.*
> *Edward Blum, legal strategist, 2021*

Commit to Action

This third stage combines the output from two Factors of the Four-Factor RACE Model, Recognise the Problem and Analyse the Impact, and challenges you to Commit to Action. So far you have shone a light on the racial issues affecting your organization. You are dedicating energy and time to your own introspective work to better understand your relationship with racism. Further, the racial inequalities exposed by your organization's data has been interrogated through root cause analysis.

Now is the time for change.

How will you and your organization solve the problems you've exposed, and most importantly, how are you going to measure your success in doing so?

Welcome to the third stage: Commit to Action.

Getting Started

Having got as far as this third factor, you're keen to get started making organization changes, so at this point does it matter if it's just you getting the ball rolling? Irrespective of where your colleagues are in their anti-racist journey, isn't it better to do something rather than nothing, and so be it if it's just you to start with. After all, at the very least, can't you get the momentum going?

> It was my decision to act. It was the right thing to do and I basically told everyone to just get on with it.
>
> Chief executive, 2020

It matters.

If you don't confront head on those leaders who are resistant to change, to doing the work and untangling their own relationship with racism, be aware of the following four scenarios that could arise.

1. **Solo efforts are difficult to sustain**.

Without your board's alignment, you will be the only person driving the anti-racism agenda. You will have limited executive input to challenge thinking, beliefs and value systems. You will be the only one your extended teams come to for direction, input, feedback and the like. And whilst initially this may not feel like a big deal, as you begin a more structured approach to becoming an anti-racist organization, this level of effort and responsibility will be very difficult to sustain.

And the impact? You will crash and burn before you've had a chance to make a difference. You'll overpromise and underdeliver, with your Black colleagues ultimately paying the price.

2. **It sends the wrong message to your colleagues**.

Whether we like it or not, we live in a permission-based society and this is how organizations are run. It is rare for employees to have true autonomy, to use their initiative and run with ideas and projects without sign-off from above.

If you are the only voice they hear talking about racism, equity and inclusion, they will quickly read between the lines. And whilst they may support and admire your stance, they will question why the other board members are so quiet and have very little or nothing to say.

And if we've learnt anything from organizations who continue to stay silent on racism, is that it speaks volumes. Silence is an action in itself that can lead to, at best, a perception that your organization is wedded to the way things are. Or, to paraphrase, provided the status quo works for the white majority, who cares what happens to everyone else.

3. **Your HR or DEI teams will be unable to do their jobs**.

For anti-racism to be taken seriously, it needs to be seen as a business-driven priority, not an HR agenda item.

Yes, you satisfy the requirement of 'it needs to be driven from the top', but it needs driven by the entire executive board, not just you.

Because when there is a need for budget, resources, time and general support, your teams need to be able to call on any board member to provide leadership in this space. How can you set them up for success if they can only talk to one person on the board – you?

How are they going to speak with the chief finance officer if the CFO can't even bring themselves to say the word 'Black'?

How can they talk about best way to engage with your wider workforce, the channels to use, the language and so on if the chief marketing/brand officer is still in the camp of 'I don't see race'?

There are only so many times you can knock on an unanswered door. The drive for your workforce to be part of the solution will inevitably wane, momentum will be lost and with it the trust and confidence in the public commitment you made to become an anti-racism organization. As a business, you stop delivering on your promises.

4. **A real yet less obvious reputational risk.**

There are increasing concerns about the fallout, which comes with saying or doing the wrong thing. This has allowed leadership teams to retreat into silence, thinking this will mitigate risk.

If you are committed to becoming anti-racist and beginning the journey, but the other board members are not engaging in the issue, are not talking about it or being part of the solution, they become the risk.

Because while you have increased your knowledge and understanding about what racism is and isn't, the nuances of language and terminology, and what you can and can't say, in what context and to whom, demonstrating an increasing confidence with a minimised risk of offending or showing casual racism through ignorance, your board have not.

And public perception is unforgiving these days. It's easier to vilify overt behaviour, whether intentional or not, because it sends a social signal that people are on the right side of the issue: 'Look at me, I condemned this racist behaviour, I took action. Demanded their resignation.' And while that is going on, no one is questioning (yet) what other steps are being taken.

Therefore, part of the action plan could be to get board alignment.

The Importance of Board Alignment

Committing to action isn't about updating a policy statement or ruminating on how to include racism in your diversity and inclusion strategy to make everything neater and easier for you.

This is a change programme and you need to treat it like one. Start with a clear and shared vision. Base it on what your version of great needs to look and feel like. Make it a vision that is centred around legacy, impact, culture and experience.

You need to have a strategy and not a to-do list. It must be incorporated into your business objectives and your values. It has to be based on understanding the root causes of why inequities and racism appear in your business. It demands leadership by you and your executive board and requires ultimate accountability.

And it needs owning by everyone in your organization.

Your teams need to be on the same page in understanding why you are taking action, what it means for them and the role they have to play. A failure to communicate the why often results in doubt and fear: fear from your Black colleagues that you are not really serious about advancing racial equity, and fear from your non-Black colleagues about what it means for them. Because don't forget, many of them will be in the same place you were: not understanding what racism is, believing they are not racist, possibly feeling resentful of the perceived attention their Black colleagues are getting, and sensing that equity means they are being left behind.

Everyone needs a job.

Board Alignment: Working on the Business, Not in It

With the multitude of business-critical priorities you have to manage, it is understandable that carving out time and headspace to address an issue that doesn't directly impact you is a challenge, particularly when there is now an expectation to address it at a strategic and operational level. Nonetheless, if you have taken on board what was covered in Recognise the Problem and Analyse the Impact, you are already in a much better place than you realise.

In starting out, CEOs and executive boards typically struggle with three key areas:

1. A lack of tools or a methodology to help them lead an anti-racism and racial equity agenda, particularly when they historically have never talked about it and lack both the professional and the lived experience to help guide them.

2. Confusion about how to demonstrate they are taking credible action beyond just hiring more Black people (despite it seeming to be the default tactical action other companies are taking)

3. Concern about how to publicly tell their story. Silence implies they are doing nothing. Sharing too much information when still working things through could look like virtue signalling.

> *We don't know what we should be doing, in what order and how. We don't feel confident, but everyone is looking to me and I don't have a clue either.*
> Diversity, equity and inclusion manager, 2021

Following are three sets of questions to consider, the answers to which will help you shape your vision and how you to approach this, together with giving your board team the time to discuss, challenge and ultimately agree on the way forward.

Setting the Vision

If you were to adopt a more progressive approach to ensure stakeholder prosperity; how could you use your brand, influence and operations to respond proactively to some of the issues affecting your colleagues, the communities you serve and the environment? Remember the stakeholder capitalism spectrum from Chapter 1? Where would you place yourself now? Or, put another way, when considering shareholder gains versus stakeholder prosperity, where would you like to sit and what will it take to get there?

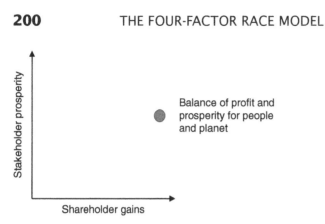

Figure 5.1   Shareholder gains versus stakeholder prosperity.

What does this shift mean for your vision, objectives, values and behaviour? Remember, you can choose the levels you put the most effort into and the answer helps determines focus, reallocation of resources and your key performance metrics.

Figure 5.2   VSOVB: Vision, Strategic Objectives, Values, Behaviour.

Where does anti-racism and racial equity fit in? One level? All of them? How?

Under Analyse the Impact, you've explored the patterns in data, the experiences of your Black colleagues and the insights from your managers and the rest of your workforce. Discuss this. What has surprised you? How do you feel about what was uncovered? How does it align with your view about how you operated as a business, as a leadership team?

What concerns you about beginning or evolving your journey to becoming an anti-racist organization? What are you afraid of? What worries you? What is the impact of those fears? How does it affect improving the experiences for your Black colleagues?

What needs to change in the way you do business to create more equity and conscious awareness of the impact of systemic racism and discrimination? Think about the expectations of your stakeholders. Do you meet, exceed or fall short?

Making It Happen: Evaluating Your Team/Resources

- What role do you each need to play? As individuals, as a business?
- What resources do you need to lead this agenda? Who do you need? What budget can you commit to?
- How can you evaluate capability to execute your plans beyond the lived experience? (In other words, don't make this the job of your Black colleagues just because they are Black.)
- What does line management accountability look like? What role are you expecting them to play? How are you going to set those expectations? How are you going to support them?

- What role should your HR, DEI teams and employee resource groups play? How are you setting them up for sustained impact?
- What measures do you need to put in place to quantify progress and impact? This is different from confirming you've done something i.e. ticked the box).
- How will you continually measure and review qualitative and quantitative patterns and trends? And how will you know when you need to intervene or change course of action?

Engaging Key Stakeholders

- Who needs to know what you're doing and why? Your customers? Workforce? Nonexecutive board? Shareholders? Suppliers? Regulators?
- How are you going to centre and involve your Black colleagues? What are their expectations of you? Are you prepared to meet that? How often will you elicit feedback directly from them?
- How will you engage your entire ecosystem? What are the new expectations they need to meet?
- What does this mean for your disclosures? How are you going to make sure you don't pander to comfort and whitewash the subject and your actions?

You don't have to go through all of these areas in one sitting. In fact I would caution against that. But perhaps you can start to see how asking the right questions will lead to a more thoughtful and thought-out approach to dismantling racism and promoting racial equity within your organization.

Additionally, the output will also give you these advantages:

- Get alignment of vision, strategic objectives, values and behaviours (top-down).
- Understand the concerns, experiences and expectations from key stakeholders and colleagues most impacted by racism (bottom-up).
- Have clarity on best next steps, whom to involve, when and why.
- Feel more in control, more confident in your ability to credibly talk about the thought process behind the actions you're taking.
- Reduce the risk of focusing on tactical actions they might sense individually, but collectively do not add up to anything meaningful in the long run.
- Understand what support you need, as individual leaders and as a collective to keep you honest and to help you push past your discomfort.

Although you may not need external support to facilitate these discussions, you do need to ensure someone can act as the voice of challenge, particularly if your team is mostly or entirely white and there is no one in the room with lived and professional experience. Otherwise, you risk retreating back to comfort, which invariably means an increased risk of making tokenistic decisions.

Ensuring Leadership Accountability

What does accountability actually mean? The word is frequently dropped into conversations and documents, but in relation to dismantling systemic racism, how should accountability show up?

In its simplest form, accountability means that you do what you say you're going to do. You take complete ownership of anti-racism and racial equity. You don't foist it onto others behind closed doors. And you show up. Consistently. Even if things don't quite go to plan.

Accountability means that you hold everyone to the same standards of conduct and behaviour. This is easy to do when taking action is linked to your values and the way you do business. Similarly, it negates the concern that becoming anti-racist and advancing racial equity should only be a concern for organizations with Black colleagues.

Accountability also means you respect the seriousness of racism, doing your best to guard against retreating back to comfort and ease and even when it happens, knowing you have the infrastructure around you to help you move past that.

It is not perfection, or the need to demonstrate deep knowledge and expertise. It is a leadership competency that should be embodied by you and anyone in your business who is responsible for leading and managing people.

The Action Plan

The whole idea of designing the plan is that you must now align the what with the how. You've interrogated your data through RCA and condensed your problem statements into a manageable number. Your board has picked up the mantle and there is leadership consensus concerning the organization's vision, strategic objectives, values and behaviours.

You are ready to put the how into place.

What action will come from your analysis, the interrogation of the whys in your problem statements? The goal is real action, not generalised 'things to do' that keep everyone doing something, but impacting nothing.

I think it is good that people are encouraged to speak up in the workplace when they experience racism or discrimination. However, it does have many repercussions and comes at a price, both financial and in mental well-being.

There is fear of repercussion over a subtle comment that wears me down and is difficult to prove (knowing I alone can understand what that comment is all about), the pitting against the only other Black person in the organization, the sudden and constant complaints about your standard of work (when they know I am a very conscientious person and want to do my best), the sudden watching of my every move (as if I cannot be trusted), feeling very much alone as my community of very few Black people who cannot help me; they are also trying to survive in the workplace and put food on the table for themselves, their family, and paying the mortgage or rent.

I know if I leave the job, and am lucky to get the next job, I cannot guarantee I will not experience the same treatment working for an organization with majority white people. I can also easily be "blacklisted" – that confidential marked letter to my next employer about me, which can start the ball of racism and other issues rolling again and again.

Yes, this is the reality of fear, and fear does not get me anywhere. But I have to weigh up the price and consequences and make decisions and choices. Do I speak up; how do I speak up; when should I not speak up at all? Do I leave the job to start on another journey and start the battle over again?

For many, speaking up means they must move jobs, and even take a job at a lower level. Time and again, speaking up means we have to leave our jobs.

Many people I have spoken to said, 'I always speak up', but when I ask if they're still there, the answer is usually no.

Colleague, 2021

Types of Change

Too often organizations reassure themselves that their action planning factors in 'race'. Remember, very few specifically use the word 'racism'. Yet when challenged on the contents, they don't go beyond generalised actions:

- Inclusion weeks
- Celebrating Black History Month
- Increasing the focus on hiring more Black people
- Partnering with inner-city schools (as if that's the only place Black students reside)
- Signing up to various race-related charters
- Purchasing new applicant tracking systems to support de-biasing recruitment
- Generic Black leadership development programmes
- Policy and procedure audits
- Unconscious bias training/education workshops

Even with your problem statements it's easy to drift back into generalised actions, because they are habitual, visually representative and externally look nice. If you find yourself heading back in this direction, keep the following in mind.

Are You Tinkering with Fish or Dredging the Lake?

'The Groundwater Approach' (Love and Hayes-Greene, 2018) is a simple metaphor concerning dying fish that aligns thinking about structural racism away from generalised action to transformative change. Although it highlights the education system, it isn't a stretch to swap out students, schools and the education system for employees, organizations and the business world in general.

It goes something like this:

If you have a lake in front of your house and one fish is floating belly-up dead, it makes sense to analyse the fish. What is wrong with it? Imagine the fish is one student failing in the education system. We'd ask: Did it study hard enough? Is it getting the support it needs at home?

But if you come out to that same lake and half the fish are floating belly-up dead, what should you do? This time you've got to analyse the lake. Imagine the lake is the education system and half the students are failing. This time we'd ask: Might the system itself be causing such consistent, unacceptable outcomes for students? If so, how?

Now. . .picture five lakes around your house, and in each and every lake half the fish are floating belly-up dead! What is it time to do? We say it's time to analyse the groundwater. How did the water in all these lakes end up with the same contamination? On the surface the lakes don't appear to be connected, but it's possible – even likely – that they are. In fact, over 95% of the freshwater on the planet is not above ground where we can see it; it is below the surface in the groundwater.

This time we can imagine half the kids in a given region are failing in the education system, half the kids suffer from ill health, half are performing poorly in the criminal justice system, half are struggling in and out of the child welfare system, and it's often the same kids in each system!

By using a "groundwater" approach, one might begin to ask these questions: Why are educators creating the same racial inequity as doctors, police officers, and child welfare workers? How might our systems be connected? Most importantly, how do we use our position(s) in one system to impact a structural racial arrangement that might be deeper than any single system? To "fix fish" or clean up one lake at a time simply won't work – all we'd do is put "fixed" fish back into toxic water or filter a lake that is quickly recontaminated by the toxic groundwater.

Love and Hayes-Greene, 2018

The issue is in the groundwater, and no amount of inclusion days, audits and unconscious bias training will detoxify the water, unless these approaches are part of a bigger solution.

Transactional and Transformative Change

Dismantling racism requires transformative change. It requires curiosity, vision and a personal commitment to make your organization as equitable and – let's be honest – as great as possible.

Transformative change is a one-to-many approach (impact will affect large volumes of people), rather than one-to-one (which affects just as a few and/or is a one-off). The purpose of taking a transformative approach is to interrogate the foundations that make up your culture, to help you decide what needs adjusting, replacing or dismantling in order to level the playing field for Black colleagues.

Too often we've focused on transactional change, meaning we've taught colleagues who are minoritised and marginalized to become better hurdlers over the structural exclusion barriers that exist. It's easier to try and fix people than it is to dismantle the barriers that stop them achieving their potential on par with other colleagues.

It's not to say there isn't a place for transactional change; it's just that you do want to over-index on it. And you certainly want to be clear on how far it is a solution to the problem for the long term versus a way to demonstrate taking action in the short term. Transactional change is the stuff – the training, the seminars – that we're all used to doing. Therefore you always need to think about balance. And the balance between the transactional and the transformative is dependent on your role, on your products and/

or services, the markets you're in and your customers, as well as the impact you want to have on the world. All of these factors determine your organization's transactional to transformational ratio.

Example: Unconscious Bias Training

Programmes like unconscious bias training aren't bad but they must lead into something more if they are to move out of performative territory to ensure they do not generate more harm than good. So you need to ask yourself, 'What specific part of the problem statement is unconscious bias training going to solve?' If the leadership team in your organization is made up entirely of white men, there's no point in running unconscious bias training because it won't unlock conversations about power, privilege and rank. It won't address why there is a lack of psychological safety within the organization, how colleagues are victimized for speaking out or why there is a reluctance to challenge the racist or discriminatory behaviour of senior leaders.

Such training won't start to address the root causes of such issues. Training a leadership team in this manner isn't going to disrupt the power dynamics, the organization's policies or systems. No one's coming out of such training any wiser when it comes to understanding the nuances of racism. Awareness of cognitive bias, yes. Action, no. Thus on its own, in this situation, unconscious bias training means nothing. And when you commit your time, energy and resources as well as your values to action, it has to mean something. It has to chip away at racial inequity. And this is why I cited unconscious bias training (without any examples of transformative action) as an example of what a Level One organization within our Racial Equity Maturity Model would over-index on.

It's not all doom and gloom for unconscious bias training, however. The question you should be asking is: How can it assist in transformative change and to what extent? It depends on the specifics of your organization, but let's say you've put in a new recruitment process that includes blind CVs, so that applicants' personal details are not included in the initial decision-making process. This sounds like a positive step forward in addressing some of the racial inequities within an organization. Yet it's transactional, because when you start interviewing and a Black female candidate comes in, your new system that incorporates blind CVs makes not a jot of difference to the conscious or subconscious racial bias of your hiring manager. Their racial bias has not been interrupted, so talent – the Black woman – is blocked from entering your workforce. On its own the new recruitment process is performative and it asks nothing of your employees, but unconscious bias training can assist with that because it can increase awareness if done consistently and regularly.

> *My biggest issue with unconscious bias training is that it's used as a catch-all to deal with all exclusionary behaviours. Unconscious bias training neither centres Black women nor deals with the systemic issues of racism and patriarchy that continually hold us back. I don't understand why organizations continue to use it as their default solution. What is it I'm missing?*
> Leanne Mair, founder and managing director,
> Benefactum Consulting, 2020

To put it another way, the issue with unconscious bias training is that organizations align it to solve the wrong problems.

It's not good for dismantling racism or solving racial discrimination, but if you have a problem trying to get people to understand why certain new policies, systems or ways of doing things have been put into place, then it has its place. It moves your 'new way of doing things' from being transactional to transformative.

This is, why when you are committing to action, the clarity of your problem statements and their root causes is essential to understanding how different tools should and shouldn't be used to dismantle racism.

Slipping into Transactional Habits

You need to keep yourself in check to ensure you're not overvaluing transactional change. Always hold this central question in your mind: 'How far does action X contribute to dismantling racism, as it manifests within our organization?'

This is a deceptively simple yet powerful leadership question that transcends the need to be an expert in racism, because you can use it when challenging the board to determine what you do or don't sign off. And in the same fashion, you can use it to challenge suppliers. Because when Black is trending, everyone claims they have a solution to the problem.

To give you control and confidence that you are making informed decisions, this is why you and your organization need to understand what systemic racism is. Because putting the solutions in place without the understanding is equivalent to going to the dentist because you have a problem with your back. You might not know why you have a back problem, but you know enough to determine that the dentist's offer of a special discount on a root canal is not the solution.

Choose Your Partners and Suppliers Carefully

Whatever you put in place has to make a difference. Therefore, the people you engage with, internally and externally, need the skills, capability and lived experience to ensure you do this in a way that doesn't perpetuate harm.

There is no point in pretending; just like any other societal problem, fixing racism is an opportunity. Intentionality also means choosing who supports you very carefully.

Some decision makers couldn't care less who supports them, provided they can help make this all go away. Other leaders feel more comfortable learning about anti-racism from white people, because it's more palatable to hear it from someone 'like them'. This feels like a safer option, particularly if there is a concern that they will be supported by someone who has a personal 'axe to grind.'

Should white-led business profit off anti-racism? That's your decision to make and it goes back to the points raised in the earlier chapters about the economic exploitation of Black people and how far you want to establish what vendors have done to tackle systemic racism within their own company.

We had a very successful and prominent culture change company lined up to help us train and introduce new leadership development programmes to become inclusive. We had done our homework, or so we thought. They appeared regularly in The Times, *you get the picture. We signed the contract and announced to our teams we were going to do this. It didn't go down well. Surprisingly, the biggest voices of dissension came from our white colleagues. They had Googled the business and found not only did they not have any Black people on their board, but there were no public commitments about where they stand in addressing racism and the company was going through a recruitment drive looking for people with 'lived experience'. Our employees felt like this was wrong. They refused to turn up to the training. This cost us a lot of money. But lessons were learnt, even though to this day I'm not sure the CEO really understands why this was such an issue.*

HR director, 2020

Challenge and make deliberate decisions every single step of the way. Start with your vision, strategic objectives, values and behaviours; think about the difference between transactional and transformational change and always keep your problem statements (not the symptoms) at the front of your mind.

Continue to ask repetitive questions. What needs one-off interventions? Where should we take a more long-term programmatic approach? How is this making a difference?

Hold colleagues, suppliers and partners accountable. Everyone is an extension of your brand values, rather than the visual representation. If racial equity matters to you and you want to take it seriously, don't knee jerk and hire or partner with the first person who promises to solve racism (no one company can do that). Don't get seduced by people who also tell you what you want to hear; that is how the system of racism keeps ticking along, through lack of challenge, prioritising of comfort and a complacency or deliberate ignorance about what's at play. This will all lead to lacklustre results.

How Are You Using Your Privilege to Create More Equity?

You can ask this deceptively simple question of your line managers, board directors, new hires, suppliers and new partners. The answer will give insight into whether their values align with yours.

Metrics

Good old metrics. The adage that what gets measured gets done is true, but only to a point.

You need to make sure your decided action has the potential to make a difference. And the metrics supporting your action plan cannot conclude solely, 'because it's the right thing to do'. This might sound strange in a book advocating for anti-racism in the workplace, but it would be naive to say the moral argument is enough for you to push through everything required, because fundamentally that would be untruthful. And to date, it hasn't worked.

Pressure to Demonstrate ROI

In achieving board sign-off on an organization's anti-racist plan, one that includes the resources necessary for success, you need to make sure what you're doing is going to make a difference, meaning that it is going to give return on investment (ROI). But the important point to realise is that the return on investment is based on how far your initiatives and the subsequent solutions positively affect the experiences of your Black colleagues. I'm saying this explicitly because in the business world, that's typically not how we are used to viewing ROI. We focus on economies of scale; therefore significant investments have to impact a significant number of colleagues over an extended period of time (in years) for said interventions to be seen as viable. If Black colleagues are the statistical minority within your organization, can you now see how that argument wouldn't stack up?

Therefore, how should you measure progress and impact?

Your anti-racist action plan is a conscious decision-making process about your impact on one of society's most persistent social issues. If you are looking for a structure to measure the ROI, you can leverage off a framework that is already embedded within business as a way of communicating disclosures and mitigating risk. You can use stakeholder capitalism metrics, as suggested by the World Economic Forum, or ESG frames, which we already know is a recognised system for reporting and disclosing ESG metrics (even if there isn't one universal framework). Whilst none of these metrics or frames will be perfect and they're not without their pitfalls, if your shareholders and stakeholders are already used to thinking about community value in terms of an ESG framework, it's a comfortable home for your anti-racism metrics. It doesn't mean you'll fit in all your metrics, but broadly speaking there are some principles within ESG reporting that could work well for your internal and external disclosures.

If you haven't spent the time setting the right metrics and ensuring you have the tools to deliver, you are increasing your organization's corporate risk. If you employ people, you cannot put 'not applicable' when drafting disclosures about the steps you are taking to diversify your executive board, for example.

Alongside your quantitative metrics you need space for qualitative detail, the positive – and negative – workplace changes as told by your Black colleagues. Not by the HR team. Not by the heads of departments. Not by self-appointed allies. You need to get the narrative of the colleagues most impacted in order to determine whether the actions you're putting in place are making a substantive difference and altering your company's cultural DNA for the better.

Think about how you can continuously put together qualitative detail, and display it alongside the quantifiable data. It's the accumulation of stories, plus data, to create insights. In doing so you're making it easier for your leadership teams to connect the dots between what's being done internally with what they need to communicate externally. It honest, transparent and authentic – something that is continually valued by colleagues, communities and customers, yet in short supply among many leaders who are nervous about the possible consequences.

Furthermore, the ability to keep reminding people of your commitment, your actions and how things are progressing means you have a better chance of maintaining the course and ultimately of creating racially just workplaces.

Confusion about What Metrics to Use

This is where the metrics for your anti-racist action plan can overlap traditional diversity, equity and inclusion measures. These measures are also an area of challenge when it comes to managing and measuring impact, and also progress, in a way that satisfies the board and what they need to disclose.

From an investor's perspective, they will always look for quantitative metrics. Where can we get data from – numbers, percentages, specific figures? This isn't to say that qualitative data should be ignored, but quantitative measures will be a strong focus when you must disclose information externally. It allows for comparisons, benchmarks and in theory the ability to compare apples with apples.

Assessing metrics for an organization is a unique process that starts from a bundle of 50–60 possible metrics and, through cherry-picking and tailoring, is narrowed down to specific requirements.

There is zero point in listing all the possible metrics because on their own they mean very little. But let's review some key metrics you might want to consider, starting with the most obvious:

Succession planning and representation at board level

Who's next? Your succession plan needs to be diversified, making sure everybody is not the same: not the same ethnicity, gender, education or socioeconomic background, in order to mitigate groupthink risk and the potentiality of poor decision-making. If everyone around the table looks like you and comes from similar backgrounds, you will all have the same perspective on the world. You will all have the same approach to business problems, which means you're less likely to see a different, innovative way to solve a problem, or even recognise an opportunity.

If you are talking about the actions you are taking and representation is the start or the forefront of your 'action', it's advisable to go back to the R of the Four-Factor Race Model: Recognise the Problem.

Beyond board level

Discernible on your website, in the media and your annual reports, your board is the most visible representation of your organization. However, how does this representation manifest itself on other structural levels?

On the back of Black Lives Matter, everyone upped the ante in ensuring there were one or two Black faces on the front of their white papers, downloadable reports, careers websites and client proposals. One would be forgiven for thinking those organizations had the same ratio of Black people within their business.

If your marketing department is getting a little too carried away with putting 'diverse faces' on the front of your internal and external collateral, gift them a copy of this book.

I'll leave it there.

Ethnicity pay gap

Just like gender pay gap reporting, it is a no-brainer that you should complete your ethnicity pay gap report and pay close attention to where your Black colleagues sit within your pay scales.

As a reminder, ethnicity pay gap shows the difference in the average hourly pay between global majority and non-global majority colleagues within your organization, as expressed by a percentage of the average non-global majority earnings. Remember, it is different from the issue of equal pay, which is about the legal requirement to pay two individuals the same for equal work (governed by the Equality Act 2010).

Employee engagement

Split the responses according to levels of seniority, according to gender within the levels of seniority, according to the ethnicity, within the seniority, so on and so forth.

Are all of your employees happy? Engaged? Feeling valued? Listened to? The majority, or just some of them? Is aggregating the data for public consumption hiding an uncomfortable truth, particularly when overlaid with attrition data and exit interview feedback (if you do them)?

Performance grades

Not every organization has a formal system for evaluating and capturing performance, but if you do, capture it, again according to seniority, gender, ethnicity and so on.

Talent management

Where are your colleagues going after they've completed your talent management programme? This is a very specific metric. If you want your talent management programme to specifically advance representation, you need to put your Black colleagues on them and then assess 'what happened next'. It is not enough to report on whether or not they've attended. It's about where they went afterwards, how many went into more senior positions, how many changed roles, how many went into other projects, how many were given stretch assignments, how many now manage their own profit and loss accounts and the like. With talent management metrics, the devil is in the details.

Turnover

What are the turnover figures, again, all broken down according to ethnicity and so on? Look at breakdowns by month and quarter, not just aggregated data for the year. Examine turnover by line manager, head of department, functional director and so on. This can tell you a lot, even if you don't publicly disclose the results.

Employee relations

How many disciplinaries or grievances, both formal and informal, relate to racism and/or racial discrimination in any given period? What were the outcomes? How did the colleagues who raised issues rate how they were supported and communicated with? Do you measure this? Would you want to?

These few examples are a mere glimpse of the vast array of metrics you can proactively put in front of investors, regulators, clients, the media, your board and your colleagues, before they ask. They are the quantitative measures stakeholders will be interested in, making you a more viable option for investment, as well as mitigating risk and attracting talent and new customers to your organization. They also give you and your executive board the information you require to demonstrate the positioning of your anti-racist action plan and whether it is advancing in line with your expectations, and those of your organization.

The Need to Demonstrate Progress Internally and Externally

Stakeholders are scrutinising organizational equity practice more than ever before. In asking, 'What are you doing?' investors, regulators, customers, employees and even competitors have moved beyond viewing the number of Black individuals you hired during your last recruitment round, even if you don't think so.

They're no longer just interested in visual representation. What they want to know about is your plan, the inputs – not just that you've got one, but whether it's credible, whether it's decisive enough. They want to know how you're going to deliver the racial equity change they need to see. However, does this level of exposure cause you and your organization transparency concerns?

If you are worried about how your public disclosures impact on confidentiality, ask yourself, 'What am I really worried about? Why am I reluctant to disclose what's really going on? What's stopping me from being transparent here?' Now, in this space true confidentiality is a myth, because you can find anything through Google and social media outlets. However, if there is ever a concern that the information you're disclosing could identify colleagues, that may compromise their safety or privacy seek legal advice.

The risk needs to be weighed. Because there's a risk inherent to withholding information regardless of whether you feel it is for legitimate reasons. And later down the line if a lender, investor or a government institution unearths the information you're purposefully withholding, they may not see your noncompliance in the same way that you did. Seek legal advice. If regulators such as the UK's Financial Conduct Authority (FCA), and financial exchanges including NASDAQ and the Toronto Stock Exchange are warning public companies to improve board representation through 'comply or explain' statements, and governments are ratifying laws that mandate board diversity, such as California's weighty AB 979, which sanctions six-figure fines (starting at $100,000 but increasing to $300,000 for each additional violation) for noncompliance, and not forgetting the ramifications to organizational reputation if you find yourself in breach, it's increasingly likely that investors, government institutions, customers and other stakeholders won't see your concealment in the same way.

Concealment is likely to be seen as complicity, so you and your organization then become an investment risk, an increasingly obsolete organization left behind in the global race for racial equity.

Always keep asking the questions. Is what we're doing making a difference? To whom? Why? And what can we learn?

Is our behaviour in line with our stated values? Do we hold each other accountable? Is our culture evolving? Are we making our workplace a safer environment for our Black colleagues to thrive?

And the final crucial question – how are we making easier for our entire workforce to be part of this? To do the right thing because they want to, not because they have to?

Empower for Change

Although Empower for Change features last in the Four-Factor RACE Model, it would be a mistake not to weave this into every stage of your anti-racism journey. Your greatest allies, supporters and pioneers are already within your workforce ready to embrace your values and an intentional path to dismantling racism. Many of them have been hoping and praying for the day you finally decided, as an executive board, to take meaningful action. They have been waiting for your leadership.

The previous three sections highlight the importance of understanding the problem and how racism manifests itself with your workplace, to collective action, executive board buy-in and advice on how to communicate progress and impact.

But how do you assist the rest of your workforce to feel like they can be part of this change? There's nothing worse than being on the sidelines, itching to help but not sure how and whether or not you are wanted. There are colleagues, of all ethnicities, who also care and are impacted by this issue, yet they are looking for explicit permission, in some cases, to lean in, roll up their sleeves and get to work.

What have you done so far to ensure all your colleagues have a better understanding of what systemic racism is, and what it isn't? How are they a part of your commitment to act? Is there a role for them? How are you upskilling them from a knowledge perspective?

What about your line managers? Your HR teams? They have a wide-angle influence on the employee experience.

How are you creating a safety net, a support infrastructure around them if you like, to give them the opportunity to practice new behaviours, to coach them, provide a confidential sounding board for them to explore their discomfort without perpetuating harm through ignorance or fear?

You cannot undo years of living under racist ideology overnight. We have all been subjected to the conditioning that comes with living within a racialised society. You cannot expect colleagues to immediately get things right.

Mistakes will happen, and your workforce needs the tools, knowledge and resources to maintain the course.

Rather than focusing on policies and procedures to catch people out, how are you making it easier for them to do the right thing? To recognise the day-to-day role they have to play, not just a blanket phrase of 'must do better' after a one-off intervention?

This is important because you cannot simply leave people in limbo just because you've 'trained' them, just because they've read something, and, you know, you've rewritten a policy so that's enough to get everyone's behaviour changed. The behavioural change that's needed is not always about whether you're not racist, or whether you say or do racist things. It's about how not to be a bystander. How you can use your voice to amplify the voices of others. How you can be an active ally. How you lead rather than follow. How you hold the organization to account. And that's got nothing to do with skin colour. This is purely about people who care.

It's up to you whether interventions, training, knowledge and upskilling should be compulsory. But for transformative change, choice is better than force. You can cut the argument in a lot of different ways, but generally there are two types of organizations when it comes to advancing racial equity. First, there are the ones who want to do something. They don't know what or how, but they're committed and just need support to get started or correct their current course of action.

And there's the other type. They don't understand why they have to do something; they need convincing that systemic racism is even a thing; they begrudgingly engage and they expect to be convinced.

If this is where your head is at, or your board colleagues, or senior leaders, it means you will struggle to get beyond

Level One – Compliance Approach – of the Racial Equity Maturity Model. All actions will be geared towards mitigating risk and ensuring you have a first line of defence if anything goes wrong.

A compliance focus isn't going to advance racial equity; all it's going to do is make sure that you can tick a few boxes to say, this is what we've done, or this is the bare minimum we'll commit to because to do anything else feels a bit too radical.

This needs to be factored into all the stages of the Four-Factor RACE model; however, the real opportunity for success or failure (as embodied by apathetic or resentful colleagues) will be driven by how you engaged with the fourth stage, Empower for Change.

Clicking Fingers, No One Comes Running

For years your Black colleagues have been ignored, undermined and underappreciated and their concerns swept under the carpet. When considering how to empower your workforce, don't do what's easiest and most convenient.

Don't ask or demand that your Black colleagues write your anti-racism statements, draft updated equity and inclusion strategies, sit in on meetings with board directors to sign off on communications, give the 'Black view' on PR and marketing, pose for your new employer brand or marketing campaign or be available for any questions about 'all this Black stuff'.

Don't metaphorically click your fingers and expect your Black colleagues to come running. This isn't how it works.

I was very disappointed to see there was a lack of enthusiasm by our Black team members. I thought they would have been grateful and pleased to get the opportunity to be part of the change. Instead we pretty much got silence. No one volunteered to be on the anti-racism task force, which feels a bit strange.

CEO, 2020

Your conversations need to centre them rather than your own fragility, or that of your majority colleagues', in advancing racial equity. Empower for Change isn't about pandering to those who feel like your actions are reverse racism or discrimination. Neither is judging the appetite for change on the wishes and demands of colleagues who are not the ones most impacted by systemic racism. This is a cycle of behaviour that has played out for centuries.

Centring white comfort never leads to progressive change.

You need to sit with the uncertainty, rather than assume your Black colleagues, because of their skin colour, will sort it all out for you. Yes, they have a vested interest in what you're doing, but this is a matter of trust.

If you historically have done very little to address incidences of overt racism, of challenging line manager decisions on who gets promoted, who is eligible for that out-of-cycle pay rise, then you cannot expect them to volunteer their time, energy and relieve their trauma, often unpaid and unrecognised, just to make your life easier.

This is real talk.

No matter how ill-prepared you start your anti-racist journey, the onus is on you to do the introspective work and get curious about the issues within your organization. This is why anti-racism and racial equity is sometimes so challenging, because we are used to operating from a place of self-interest, taking actions that directly improve things for us, or the majority. Here, you and your peers will be required to do the heavy lifting, knowing that the payoff won't be immediate, there is no gold star or certificate of recognition at the end and your Black colleagues are not going to trip over themselves in gratitude.

If you really want the public recognition to help keep you all going, there are plenty of diversity and inclusion awards going that pretty much give everyone a pat on the back for showing up.

That is the reality.

At the forefront of your mind, be aware that any support you request you should approach from a position of listening and not demanding. Find what support your Black colleagues need, if they are willing and able to help, how their workload will be adjusted accordingly, how they will be recognised and compensated for their part, how expansive is their sphere of influence and what budget they have at their disposal.

And ensure they do not become the single point of failure for projects.

Bear all of this in mind when recruiting heads of diversity and inclusion with the lived experience.

Active Allyship

I deliberately have not centred the book on allyship, yet it is an important part of anti-racism, particularly when you do not have the power and influence associated with your rank, job title or position within your organization.

How can you make active allyship for yourself, and your colleagues, a real thing rather than something everyone nods their head to without truly understanding what it means? How do you make sure it is truly active, as the verb, and carries momentum, allowing the right supportive behaviours to show up day in and day out?

There are practicalities to consider when it comes to active allyship. It's one thing to read a book or attend a seminar and quite another putting it into practice.

> *I was told that I couldn't give feedback, that colleagues felt uncomfortable with the language used by the functional director. How can we roll out training on allyship, if I'm banned from speaking up about poor behaviour just because the person concerned is a director? It makes no sense and frustrates the hell of out me."*
> HR business partner and inclusion lead, 2020

Speaking truth to power, no matter who you are, is very difficult. Everyone is so used to shying away from conversations about racism, so very few of us have built the confidence muscles to be able to consistently speak out when they notice something isn't right. But it's only in speaking out and sometimes not quite getting it right that you get better. In this case practice doesn't make perfect, but it will increase your confidence.

Allyship isn't about charity. Remember, because of our skin colour and where society places us, there are ways in which you can intervene that we as Black people can't. This is not to say that we can't speak up, but the implications and the consequences for us are very different in comparison to the consequences for you.

To narrow allyship from the abstract to the practical, consider the following.

Be Prepared   Prepare some things to say in case an incident happens; for example, you're in a meeting and you've noticed that a Black colleague is talked over, or when they make a contribution to the conversation it's somehow missed. And then when somebody else makes the same suggestion everyone listens and praises the individual for their contribution. Think about how you would interrupt that meeting. How could you step up and ensure credit is given where credit is due?

You can't control what someone else says, but you can control what you say.

Or maybe you have witnessed somebody interact with a Black colleague in a way that's questionable. Sometimes when white colleagues are trying to grapple with racism they find it difficult to calibrate their worldview with someone who has experienced racism. So their questions are more akin to an interrogation. There's a tone, sometimes an aggression that implies their Black colleague has to prove systemic racism to them, that racism is a thing. That they should be able to run off all the stats, the data points and be able to articulate it. And if they don't agree, then the onus is, again, on the Black colleague to educate them. But it's coming from a place of 'I don't believe you'. Now, in that scenario – and it plays out often – if you're witnessing this, or you happen to overhear this exchange, how would you intervene? After all, Google is free and it's not the burden of Black people to educate everyone else on the nuances of racism. But gaslighting and tone policing are also not okay, even if there was no harm intended. (See Chapter 3 for details on terminology.)

In the Moment   Address the issue in the moment. There's nothing worse than people commenting on things after the fact. And again, this is only something that's relevant for overt racist behaviour or when you feel like somebody is out of order. Your input doesn't have to be adversarial; it can be as simple as, 'Listen, I don't know if you meant to come across this way. But let me tell you, this is how you sounded', or 'I don't know if you meant offence, but actually some of the things you said here are really questionable.' They might engage in a conversation with you.

And there is nothing wrong with saying, 'Just before I comment, can I clarify what you meant?' or 'Can I just play back my interpretation of what you're saying?' or even 'Where does this belief you have come from? And what makes you so certain that your view of the world is correct?'

Focusing on Intent Within organizations there is bias towards intent, that white people don't mean it when they say X, or when they've done Y.

A greater focus on impact is required.

Someone doing something that wasn't intentional shouldn't be excused from taking responsibility. That it wasn't intentional is not the point; the impact that it's had on a Black colleague is. So being an active ally is catching yourself when you're trying to excuse the behaviour of people who look like you, because you like them, because you know them, because they 'don't have a bad bone in their body'.

It's instinctive for us to step into protection mode with people we like and people we know. But every time you do that, you're censoring the individuals impacted, and you're not attempting to see things from their point of view.

Defensiveness Not every colleague is going to be open and have the growth mindset to hear constructive feedback. Some will work hard to defend their view of the world. They will work hard to defend the fact they didn't mean X, Y and Z. This is where conversations turn to, 'I understand that you are really uncomfortable with that, but part of changing the culture of our organization is about addressing how we interact with each other. That our interaction comes from a true place of respect from empathy and compassion. And I need you to hear me, and not try to fight me on this, but just hear me. And even if you disagree, that's fine. But at least I want to know that I've pointed out something that doesn't sit right with me.'

In these situations it's okay to say that you're not an expert in racism or what it means to be Black. That you can only talk about your experiences from your perspectives, using the power and privilege you have, that your Black colleagues don't, to intervene when you think something's not right.

In doing so you're taking control of the conversation, all the time being mindful that as an ally you have to have challenging patience, which means you have to give people the space to talk out and to respond when you're challenging them on their behaviour, whether it's something they've said, something they've done, something they've written or the tone in which they've said certain things. In the spirit of safety netting (if that's even a phrase), give people the chance to correct their words. Don't shy away from the impact; give them the chance to atone and remember that the real apology is owed to the colleague who was adversely impacted by their behaviour. An apology to you doesn't count.

The Flip Side   If you intervene and your Black colleague is with you or in the room, ensure you are not speaking over them or on their behalf, assuming that they can't speak for themselves. Give them the option to join the conversation or if their body language implies they would rather not be part of the conversation, read that and respect it. Don't take it personally. And refrain from implying that next time you 'won't bother'.

This isn't about seeking external validation and recognition, the self-appointed badges of allyship. This is about making a difference and making a difference in the way that your Black colleagues prefer – with their preferences being centred, not yours.

Final Thoughts on the Four-Factor RACE Model

Every action you take under each of the Four Factors of the RACE Model is going to differ depending on the size and scale of your operations and on your line of business. It also depends on how connected your leadership teams are to dismantling racism, and how many Black colleagues you have in your organization. Irrespective of your organization's specifics, it doesn't mean you shouldn't or can't do anything to effect change.

References

Koenig, Melissa. (9 September 2021). AmEx employees allege the company engages in 'reverse discrimination'. Retrieved 15 September 2021, from https://www.dailymail.co.uk/news/article-9974133/Former-current-American-Express-employees-allege-company-engages-reverse-discrimination.html.

Lewis, Keith. (9 September 2021). SEC-backed Nasdaq rule on diversity faces court challenge – Roll Call. Retrieved 15 September 2021, from https://www.rollcall.com/2021/09/09/sec-backed-nasdaq-rule-on-diversity-faces-court-challenge/.

Love, Bayard, and Hayes-Greene, Deena. (2018). The Groundwater Approach: Building a Practical Understanding of Structural Racism. Racial Equity Institute. https://www.racialequityinstitute.com/groundwater.

A Sustainable Future Needs Equity at the Heart

The wealth gap between American whites and Blacks is projected to cost the US economy between $1 trillion and $1.5 trillion in lost consumption and investment between 2019 and 2028. This translates to a projected GDP penalty of 4 to 6 percent in 2028.

Losavio, 2021

In France GDP could jump 1.5 percent over the next 20 years – an economic bonus of $3.6 billion – by reducing racial gaps in access to employment, work hours, and education.

Bon-Maury et al., 2016, cited in Losavio, 2021

Opinions and perspectives about what it means to be a sustainable organization are now commonplace. Traditionally, sustainability was associated with the environment, your green credentials, but over time it has become much more than that.

You could be forgiven for assuming I would immediately lead with a lofty and somewhat predictable declaration that anti-racism and racial equity need to be at the forefront of sustainability. Yet my view of what a truly sustainable business means is simple: one that does business consciously aware of its impact on colleagues, the environment, the community or society as a whole. This is encapsulated with the traits and values shared between the Sustainable Development Goals, as championed by the United Nations and robust ESG frameworks and evolved stakeholder capitalism approaches.

If 2020 proved anything it was that our world is getting smaller, so your community is now not just local or regional but global, irrespective of where your offices and people are. This is why I coined the phrase 'global race to equality'. It truly is global.

To commit to sustainability means you can't shy away from tackling the issues that are barriers to opportunities, and that marginalise, exclude and silence. Even if it makes you feel uncomfortable. Even if you're worried about the reputational risk of saying and doing the wrong thing. Even if you just can't be bothered and you actually feel like it's better just to ban any conversations that remotely seem too political, as determined by your own comfort level. But remember, the political issue of racism is social because it's systemic in our society, deeply ingrained in the way we think, act and speak.

It isn't just about how much more productivity you can squeeze out of Black people either. It isn't about homing in on the economic and profit-driven advantages that come with diversifying your teams across the board as the justification to act. It's about recognising that systems underpinning our society are man-made. They didn't just appear; they were designed that way: a combination of self-serving decision-making and the collective action or inaction and wishes and demands of individuals.

Therefore one of the objectives of a sustainable business is to make a positive impact on society, and that's where anti-racism and racial equity come in. It's one that uses culture as an opportunity for positive change, and recognises there should be a laser focus on anything that negatively impacts how colleagues are treated in the workplace, and acknowledges that it's okay to put interventions in place that on the surface prioritise the 'minority' over the 'majority'.

A sustainable organization has workplace cultures that could be described as playdough. You can continually shape them to meet the needs of your colleagues, and by meeting their needs you can keep yourself in check that you're not making decisions that merely suit your comfort levels or those of your executive board. The sustainable organization within the playdough analogy allows your teams to co-shape your culture, according to what they need to bring their best selves – their best ideas, creativity and productivity – and not what's easiest for you.

The caution is that if you have homogeneous teams across the entire organization or in decision-making roles, those individuals are likely wedded to creating cultures that work best for them and those who look like them. It may not be deliberate, but the lack of Black colleagues in senior roles, for example, did not happen by accident.

This is why setting an intentional direction, leading with a clear vision, is so important. If you leave it to happen by accident, you won't get the result you – or wider society – requires.

Aim for nothing, hit nothing.

Dismantling systemic racism comes under the banner of your vision of a sustainable organization.

Challenge the concept of normal in your workplace. Consider how you can educate your customers to think differently about some of the world's biggest problems, particularly if you're worried that by engaging in anti-racism you'll alienate your most profitable clients. However, with the way the world is headed, if you don't change, the ramifications are increasingly profound. Your sustainability credentials, typically housed in annual reports or shareholder updates, is open to challenge, if you cannot address how you are monitoring the impact of the way you do business to ensure that chasing short-term profits don't turn into long-term liabilities.

By 2021 **86% of people responding to the annual Edelman Trust Barometer (Edelman, 2021) expect CEOs to publicly speak out about societal challenges,** with **68% agreeing that CEOs should step in when governments do not fix societal problems.** When this doesn't happen through their own volition, **68% of consumers and 62% of employees expect to have the power to force organizations to change.**

CEOs should hold themselves accountable to the public and not just to the board of directors or stockholders - 65% of respondents.

Edelman, 2021, p. 34

Beyond the moral argument it's just good business sense.

Getting It Right

Everyone wants to know who is doing it better: who the competition is, who can they learn from and compare themselves to and how that knowledge can be a catalyst to do more.

Are there organizations currently achieving sustainability with authentic progress in dismantling racism? Although there are CEOs and organizations making huge inroads in this space, no one has got this nailed.

Some organizations, due to the sheer scale of their operations, are able to commit to a lot of transformative change, because they have the money, influence, scale and international footprint to get involved with social justice and extended community endeavours.

If you're a small company, external transformative change on this scale is not on your radar and probably feels very scary. But part of sustainability and advancing racial equity is thinking about what you *can* do, within your scope of influence.

How can you ensure that you're not perpetuating racism, or reinforcing the idea that whiteness as a social construct is normal? For example, what process do suppliers you work with have to go through to win your business? Are there inherent assumptions or structural barriers within that process? This is your equivalent to the external action taken by some of the largest organizations around the globe.

And remember, the external image doesn't always reflect the internal reality for Black colleagues. Some of these organizations are atoning for their direct history in oppressing Black people, of commercially benefiting from the school to prison pipeline or playing an active role in the slave trade. There are organizations within the UK whose founding fathers were compensated by the UK government because they had to relinquish their plantations and 'free' their slaves. In fact, it was only in 2015 that the British taxpayer finished 'paying off' the debt that the British government incurred when paying British slave owners in 1835 because of the abolition of slavery. Some organizations have unblemished records externally, but the walls are talking and they tell a different story.

Focus on Your Lake

Concentrate on your lake (see Chapter 5) and ask yourself: How can you use your presence and what you do as an opportunity to lobby for transformational change? How can you support others who are doing the real work? Who can you connect them to? What spaces can you invite them into? How can you practice equity in all the different variations of your ecosystem?

If your building uses a contract cleaning company, for example, how are those colleagues treated? You are the client; use your voice and influence to ask the questions that keeps racial equity on the radar.

Use the insights that you have and the network that you are a part of to make a difference in terms of social impact – even if they are not, nor ever will be, your customers or potential new hires.

Keep asking the questions. That's how we divest ourselves of ignorance.

Out of all the answers, make an informed decision about what you and your teams collectively feel will have the most impact in the short, medium and long term. What do we feel is in keeping with our values so much so that we absolutely would love to do something about it? If you continue to centre colleagues, customers and community members who are most impacted, you are a genuine enabler of change.

The main question to keep in mind throughout all of this, to reiterate from earlier, is this: How does your action fundamentally disrupt the system of racism?

- Is what we're doing raising awareness?
- Is it giving us a better understanding of the problem?
- Does it help us understand the root causes of inequities?
- Is it equipping us with the tools and expertise to act?
- Is it empowering our entire workforce to be pioneers of change?
- Is it making a difference? For our Black colleagues, based on what they tell us, not what we want to believe. Or is it just making us feel good?

But I think people can see the change that we're making because I was talking to one of my colleagues at work and she said, 'We do actually see everything you're doing and we know that sometimes you come up against resistance, but we can see that you're still at it every day. You're pushing for us. And we do see it. And we do talk amongst ourselves.'

Participant in the HR rewired Racial Equity Development Lab Accelerator, 2021

The Final 10

I wanted to summarise some key principles weaved through-out the previous chapters as a way to solidify what you've learnt and help you think more expansively about how you recalibrate your approach to dismantling systemic racism within your workplace. This is an opportunity to transform individuals and teams, forging stronger relationships built upon authentic and equitable foundations, not feeling paralysed by fear, discomfort and guilt.

These are the ten principles to remember in creating your ultimate anti-racist organization:

1. People most impacted should be able to participate and be consulted on the solutions – through choice, not force.
2. It is the responsibility of the organization to maintain order – think structures, accountability, and the like – and the responsibility of the community, your teams, to abide by the values and behavioural expectations that have been set.
3. It is essential to set problem statements that are anchored in root cause analysis. Be relentless in tackling the cause, not passively addressing the symptoms.
4. Insist on universal clarity on the problems to be solved. This is imperative if you are to make an informed decisions about the solutions and guard against wasting time, money, energy and resources on actions that make very little to no difference.
5. Progress must be measured by impact and the extent to which you have made a difference, not whether you've

ticked off action points on your diversity and inclusion to-do list.

6. Be prepared to play the long game and recognise the trade-off between long-term impact and short-term ROI.

7. Feeling fatigued, frustrated and disengaged is common. I wish it wasn't so, but as human beings it is hard to work tirelessly for something that doesn't directly impact us. Dismantling systemic racism needs a different level of tenacity, optimism and fearlessness.

8. There is no such thing as a static goalpost. What constitutes a success today may be perceived as subpar tomorrow. Be adaptable and focus on the vision of what you're trying to achieve, not the recognition of what you've done so far.

9. The change in business climate has seen us move from 'should we diversify' to 'how fast can we do so?' Case point: a lack of representation highlights a problem; it doesn't tell you the cause.

10. People will make mistakes and get it wrong at times, yet that isn't a pass to excuse racist and discriminatory behaviour. We've moved on from focusing on intent, and prioritizing white comfort. Just because someone didn't mean it or were unaware doesn't equate to not holding them accountable.

Support Your Leaders to Continue Their Journey

Explore several ways for you, your business and people leaders to engage with key themes and reflective questions covered within the book. Visit www.shereen-daniels.com for more downloadable resources.

References

Edelman, Richard. (23 June 2021). Trust, the Brand New Entity. https://www.edelman.com/trust/2021-brand-trust/brand-equity.

Losavio, Joseph. (Fall 2021). What Racism Costs Us All. Retrieved 15 September 2021, from https://www.imf.org/external/pubs/ft/fandd/2020/09/the-economic-cost-of-racism-losavio.htm.

Tax Justice Networks (2020). Britain's Slave Owner Compensation Loan, reparations and tax havenry. Retrieved 11 January 2021, from https://taxjustice.net/2020/06/09/slavery-compensation-uk-questions/

Where Do We Go from Here?

We've come to the end of this book.

It would be very easy for me to give you a summary of all the things we've covered: talking about the inside work that's needed, reminding you to take the time to align your board, to analyse data and be clear on metrics, all the while reminding you that the Four-Factor RACE model is not linear. It's merely a framework to help make sense of what can feel very scary and abstract at times.

Instead, I'd like to take you on a brief diversion, just for a moment.

Pause and think about where we are in the world right now. Think about what's happened in the last few months, years, decades and even centuries.

Is this our chance to genuinely understand a little bit more about the systemic elements of racism, about challenging our language, our belief systems, our values, and begin to proactively question *why* things are the way they are, rather than act as passive bystanders? In way we have never been able to do so before?

It strikes me that throughout this book we are fundamentally talking about humanising the impact of racism. Reminding you of what could be the basic need for everyone to be supported to exceed their potential, to feel happy at work, productive, safe and feel like they matter.

Many months ago, I came across a post on Instagram. I have no idea who wrote it (it was one of those black background and white text affairs), but the power in this simple question has stuck with me ever since:

Might we want to emotionally divest from knowing the truth?

We are raised to be logical beings. To favour what we can see, touch with an ability to rationalise away what seems impossible and implausible.

We get hung up in wanting proof, beyond reasonable doubt in a criminal justice sense, or within the balance of probabilities in an employment law sense. Looking to 'strip away the emotion' and deal only with the 'facts' is a commonly heard phrase, as if emotion is inherently a bad thing.

Yet here is my belief. The tendency to focus and refocus on uncovering the facts of a situation, of a phenomenon, of a societal issue that even now many of us still don't fully understand, ultimately distracts us from seeing people for who they are, not who we perceive them to be, and thus it becomes impossible to give them what they need when they ask for help.

Does it need to be any more complicated than that? Do you need protests, regulation, force and compliance to make decisions that can radically improve the experiences for Black colleagues within your workplace?

What is it that your teams need to thrive? What is it that they need to feel happy? What is it that they need to feel productive? Supported? Safe?

Therefore, if you're saying your people are genuinely the heartbeat of your organization, does your incessant commitment to facts, homing in on details, truly matter? Don't your teams matter more?

Instead, could you and executive teams make a pact of some sort? One that says, if these issues matter to our colleagues, irrespective of how few of them there may be, do we not owe it to them to do as much as we can to remove the barriers that stop them from contributing, from being seen, heard and appreciated? Does it matter that we still don't quite fully comprehend how we got here? That we don't agree that we are privileged and have more power and influence because of how society values those who look like us?

Can we do away with needing proof, data that validates our colleagues lived experience to convince us to act? Instead, can we utilize data to show us where to start?

Can we acknowledge that pressuring people to validate their lived experience – whether it is about their racial identity or other identities and characteristics that make up who they are – is reinforcing our power, our truths and therefore we become part of the system called racism, destined to keep doing the work is was originally designed to do. Because what we're saying is their lives don't matter unless *we* validate it. And who are we anyway? Are we saying that our lives matter more than theirs?

You may create your own version of a leadership pact, but can you see how it can be a powerful way of pushing past your discomfort to act? Because when people speak out, it is because they want to be heard. Your colleagues are telling you that they're unfairly victimized by a system none of us created but that all of us have a role in upholding; that they're impacted by what's happening in society; that they're impacted by the behaviours of their colleagues, their line managers, their directors; that they're impacted by apathy and silence about issues that affect them, and the communities they are part of. And when you focus solely on trying to get to the facts, you're shutting down a part of them that so desperately wants to belong, that wants not to have to fight to be heard, not to have to work twice as hard and still be overlooked.

You are reinforcing exclusion.

When I spoke through my first video (available on YouTube at https://tinyurl.com/DanielsDayOne) in May 2020 that brought me here, I so desperately wanted to be heard. But more importantly, I didn't want people to be able to un-see me, to un-see who I am, what I stand for and why this matters.

Why I matter.

By emotionally divesting from the truth, what we're saying is, 'It doesn't matter whether I 100% know the facts. It doesn't matter whether I 100% understand where you're coming from; what I do understand is that if you're speaking out about something, it is my responsibility to pay attention'. And from an organizational perspective, what you're saying is, 'If our people are telling us, "This is how we feel", as a collective it is our responsibility to listen and take action'.

Too often we get caught up in the need for proof to validate or to de-risk the actions we want to take. Yet in doing so, we continually make it about us, never about the people who are most impacted.

Often the human experience is not made up of true knowledge in the literal sense. We are all a messy, beautiful combination of emotions, experiences, memories, hopes, dreams, fears and aspirations. We've all been taught to value facts, practicality, detail, validation, objectivity, logic and reasoning above all else. Thus, in the absence of all of that, we can never be taken seriously – as individuals, as leaders, as a collective within a progressive organization. And that scares us.

My journey over the last few years that has culminated in me writing this book is the antithesis of what not to do in business. Of what not to do if you want to be taken seriously as a Black woman operating in majority white spaces. Of what not to do if you want to keep white people on side and not make them feel uncomfortable, because then you'll have no chance. I've been told this over and over again.

What is it I'm not meant to do? Talk about racism. I've done it anyway – through choice, despite the attacks, the warnings and the abuse in some instances. Do we really want to live in a society that has to use force to get people to do the right thing, and that reinforces historical power dynamics in present-day decision-making? Do you want a leadership legacy that points to you taking action because you felt you had no choice? Is that who we've become? Who you've become?

An alternative is to think about what it would take to shift your culture to one that appreciates and values individuals for who they are, yet also recognises that the world is not fair, opportunities are unequal and racism is a real thing, and therefore moral courage, humility and tenacity are a few of the leadership competencies that are essential in being able to authentically respond to whatever obstacles you face as your business grows or as you service a greater number of customers.

What would it take to look and really see the impact of how society is constructed? What would it take for you to question why there are still consistent favourable outcomes for some and consistent unfavourable outcomes for others? What would it take to shift your way to thinking to realise that the impact of racist behaviour – rather than intent – is what's important? That not everything is logical and objective, yet this shouldn't stop you prioritising your colleagues as individuals, even if they are the statistical minority within your organization.

When all is said and done, what are we really left with?

Human beings who just want to feel part of the organization that they work for. Human beings who just want to feel like their lives are as valid as everyone else's. Human beings who want to feel like they're enough. That our lived experience is enough. That we can move away from having to parade our trauma over and over again as the only way to raise awareness because even when presented with evidence, that somehow still isn't enough.

That when we speak someone will listen.

I wish people like me didn't have to fight for others to see our humanity.

In the end, it boils down to choice.

What you choose to do after reading this book is completely up to you.

> *What will it take for us to trust each other with what we need, instead of continually having to prove that we need it?*
>
> Anon

Index